NOT ANOTHER F-ING MOTIVATION BOOK

A PRAGMATIST'S GUIDE TO NAILING YOUR MOTIVATION, KEEPING IT, AND EFFORTLESSLY ACHIEVING YOUR GOALS

JOANNA JAST

CONTENTS

PART IV

POPULAR MOTIVATIONAL STRATEGIES AND HOW TO USE THEM

NOT ANOTHER F-ING MOTIVATION BOOK

A Pragmatist's Guide to Nailing Your Motivation, Keeping It, and Effortlessly Achieving Your Goals

by

Joanna Jast

Disclaimer

The information in this book is intended for educational and informational purposes only and should not be taken as expert instructions or commands. It should not be treated as advice or as a substitute for seeking help from an appropriately trained health professional or expert. While all attempts have been made to verify the information provided in this book at the time of writing, the author and publisher do not assume any responsibility for errors, omissions, or contrary interpretations of the subject matter herein. The author and publisher therefore disclaim any liability to any party for any loss, damage, or disruption caused by errors or omissions, whether such errors or omissions result from negligence, accident, or other cause. Adherence to all applicable laws and regulations, including international, national, federal, local, professional licensing, business practices, educational advertising and all other aspects of doing business under any jurisdiction is the sole responsibility of the purchaser or the reader.

Neither the author nor the publisher assumes any responsibility or liability whatsoever on behalf of the purchaser or reader of these materials.

The fact that an organisation or a website is referred to in this work as a citation or a potential source of further information does not mean the author or the publisher endorses the information the organisation or website may provide or recommendations it may make. Further, readers should be aware that Internet websites listed in this work may have changed or disappeared between when this work was written and when it is read.

Any perceived slight of any individual or organisation is purely unintentional. Names and characters of the persons presented in the book have been changed to protect their privacy.

The author made every effort to accurately represent the strategies in this work, but examples used should not be interpreted as a promise or guarantee.

The examples within this book are not intended to represent or guarantee that everyone or anyone will achieve their desired results. Each individual's success will be determined by his or her circumstances, desire, dedication, effort and motivation.

❀ Created with Vellum

YOUR FREE GIFT

In order to get the most out of *Not Another F-ing Motivation Book* I've created a free workbook, which will guide you through the steps needed to create your own powerful source of motivation.

Download your accompanying FREE workbook today by going to www.theshapeshiftersclub.com/motivationworkbook

INTRODUCTION

"Thank Goodness there is tomorrow - I can start over."

— Anon quoted from memory

This is one of the many motivational quotes I had on my wall when I was a second-year medical student. I found it in a book, or an article, or maybe an inspirational poster (I had a nice collection at that time). I really liked it. I thought it was hope-instilling. I believed it would push me to work on my goals harder, to study, exercise, eat less, be a better person ...

Yeah, right.

At some point, my fantastic friend, *E*, with whom I was flat-sharing at the time, suggested that I put the quote on the ceiling.

'Every morning when you wake up, this note will be the first thing you see. And then you can just relax, thinking: thank goodness, I don't have to nail it today - I can start over tomorrow.'

We both laughed, but I realised that sadly, *E* had a point (she often did). Despite all those fantastic quotes, visualisations of success, accountability buddies, and promises given to myself and other people, my life was a total mess. I couldn't muster enough energy to study. I was walking out of lectures or skipping them completely because I found them boring. My eating habits were worse than ever (I basically lived on sweets), I was piling on weight; my sleep was all over the place. In short, I hated my life.

Believe me I tried to change that—reading all those motivational quotes, reminding myself of good things I would be able to do for people once I become a doctor, visualising myself saving lives. Of course, I wanted to achieve it. Of course, I wanted to make the world a better place. Unfortunately ...

I still felt as stuck as I'd ever been. My grades were barely passable, despite all the hours I was putting in. My day-night rhythm was upside down as I stayed up late trying to study. I was stuffing my face with sweets to keep going and 'boost my motivation'. My brain was so tired, I couldn't think straight in the mornings. I started suffering migraines—sometimes for days on end.

I felt powerless, inadequate, misplaced, a failure. All I wanted was my Fairy Godmother to come and wave a magic wand and make it all better.

This is usually the point in the story where you hear how something inspired the protagonist to turn their life around. It's usually a profound experience, a wake-up call, a world-shattering conversation with someone, an epiphany. I'd love to write this was the case with me, but ... it wasn't.

One day, I returned home from the university, having just earned a 'C-' on a test, for which I had studied several nights. It wasn't bad—some of my classmates failed outright—but I cried. I felt completely shattered, exhausted, and confused why my efforts had not brought the results I truly wanted. What was wrong with me? Was I too stupid to become a doctor? Was I not dedicated enough?

I saw the grade as a failure, and it hurt. But what really got me down was the realisation that even though the people around me were not necessarily smarter or more motivated, they were driven by a different force. It was the desire to become doctors, save lives, and alleviate suffering that was fuelling their efforts. And me? I pictured myself doing the same. I thought of all the ways I could make the world a better place. But no matter how hard I tried, it didn't resonate with me, it didn't set my heart on fire, didn't make me feel as though I could move mountains.

Deep down, at the bottom of my heart, all I wanted to do was to create beautiful things for people to enjoy: music, poetry, neatly resolved stories ...

I got so angry with myself, I ripped all the motivational quotes off the wall.

I didn't start rebuilding my life until a few months later. I did have a few moments of epiphany, some of them ridiculously simple (like discovering that I was much less inclined to fall asleep during my study session if I did it in the morning and at my desk, than in the evening/night and on the sofa/bed), some embarrassing (eh, no ... I won't tell you :-))

But at some point, I started to realise that there was something wrong with my motivation. At the time, I wasn't sure what it was, but I felt that none of the typical motivational strategies would help me turn my life around.

It took me about 20 years to get to the bottom of this, but I finally did.

Over the past few years I've become acutely aware that mainstream motivational strategies are inadequate and ineffective, not only for me, but for many others, even though some people seem to thrive on them.

It is as though there is a one set of rules governing motivation for some of us, and a completely different set for others. How annoying!

Sadly, there is a darker side to it—because if you can't achieve your goals, you not only feel like a failure, people question if you even care about your goals.

And if you speak to motivational gurus, if you read their books and articles, listen to their podcasts and motivational speeches, you may see a pattern. They'll say something like: 'This is the way to go and if it doesn't work for you—well, you need to try harder. Because if you don't—you're a loser, there is something wrong with your motivation and ... worst of all—there is something wrong with you.'

But more and more people are becoming aware that what has been served up as motivational advice for years may not always work for everyone. There is also evidence emerging that some of those classic approaches may not be as effective as experts in the field originally thought.

So, just because you happen to function differently, you don't have to feel like a failure anymore.

You don't have to motivate yourself harder. You don't have to waste energy on strategies that never last long. You don't have to live up to high and lofty standards some 'gurus' say you do. Motivation comes in many shapes and sizes. One size most definitely doesn't fit all.

So, what can you do?

If you want a proven, but less 'cookie cutter' approach to finding your motivation and keeping it for good, this book is for you.

Let me just repeat that. Ahem.

If you want a proven, but less 'cookie cutter' approach to finding your motivation and keeping it for good, this book is for you.

Sounds good? Read on.

In this book, I'm going to show you a framework that will help you:

- see how motivation really works (according to the current state of the knowledge)
- discover what really motivates you and plug into that potent source of power
- ensure that whatever goal you pursue is aligned with your motivation, so you always work towards your goals and not against them, or against yourself
- create a goal-achievement plan that is fuelled by the most powerful and ever-lasting motivation you can find in yourself (however little you think you have)
- ensure that your motivation tank is topped up without having to 'motivate yourself'
- determine which motivational strategies are likely to work for you in specific situations so you don't waste your time and energy on trying things that are unlikely to work for you.

The content of the book is organised in a logical, step-by-step way, that allows you to:

- discover what really motivates you,
- understand how best to use your motivation to achieve your goals, and
- understand how to keep your motivational fuel 'topped up' without going through the exhausting 'motivate yourself' cycles.

How do I know this approach works?

After many years of using what were, for me, the wrong motivational tools, I run regularly, even though I hate running. My diet is healthy. I have lost some weight (almost effortlessly recently). I have success-fully completed an MBA and a sought-after English teaching qualifi-cation, mastered French to a fluent level, published a couple of best sellers and all that–without a single motivational quote!

In my nearly 20 years of practice as a psychiatrist and psychothera-pist, as well as in my Shapeshifters Club business I have also helped many people discover their true motivation and build strategies and systems to keep them going on their way to long-term goals.

Did I discover the recipe for a magic motivation-boosting potion?

No, not at all.

My motivation still waxes and wanes. There are days where I have to drag myself to my desk. About 70% of the time I don't want to go for a run. But, I still write and run regularly, as per my schedules.

If you, too, struggle with motivation regardless of all the visualisation you do, accountability buddies you sign up with, reward-dishing apps you buy, I've got a message for you.

If the classic strategies described in motivational books have not helped you in the past, then, the likelihood is, they are not going to help you now. And if you keep doing the same thing over and over, you'll keep getting the same poor result—you will continue to lapse and struggle and feel like a failure.

But this book can change it for you. The strategies I share have trans-formed my, and many other people's lives. These strategies have made us more successful, happier, healthier and wealthier, and can do the same for you.

If you want to achieve long-term goals, whether personal or profes-sional, if you truly want to transform your life—keep reading.

Whether you are a complete beginner or someone who has tried and failed many times, in this book, you will find strategies and tricks that can help you discover what your true motivation is, plug into it, and drive it, without ever feeling you need to 'motivate yourself' again.

This book is for people who:

- have tried to achieve a long-term goal but failed because they 'ran out of motivation'
- have tried traditional motivational strategies without sustained effect
- are tired of blanket 'get motivated' advice.

If any of these describe you, keep reading.

This book will show you how to tackle these problems and achieve your long-term goals faster, with less effort and more enjoyment, so you can achieve that professional and/or personal success you deserve.

Are you ready to transform your life with the least energy necessary?

Turn the page.

WHAT THIS BOOK IS AND WHAT IT IS NOT

OK, I admit it —this *is* a motivation book, but it's different from the ones you usually find on the shelves with self-help literature. I don't swear here (you've been warned!), but I do challenge many well-established motivational approaches, showing how and why they may not work for everyone.

I also present alternative strategies for ensuring that your motivation lasts and you achieve your goals. I talk more about my approach in the ensuing chapters.

Before I move on, I wanted to tell you what this book is not, so that if you're looking for any of these, you can stop reading right now. I don't want you to waste your time or money on something that is unlikely to help you.

There you go, I've put it right up front. 😄

There are no motivational quotes or inspirational stories in this book. You may feel inspired and motivated by the stories I share here, but the main point of me telling you all these things is to illustrate the point, not to inspire. In libraries and bookshops you'll find mountains of books that offer you this type of content, but this is not one of them.

I use examples from my own life, and experiences of people I've worked or talked with. I also use research. Yes, there are stories, examples and studies that challenge my point of view. I know. The point is not to prove anyone wrong or right, but to show alternative motivational strategies for those of us (you) who have tried these popular approaches and have failed many times.

Again, this is not to say that the strategies I suggest will definitely work for you, because they may not. The point of this book is to help you see alternatives. It is up to you to test them and decide whether they work for you.

Ah, and since we're at it, I just wanted to make it clear that the level of your success in 'nailing' your motivation and achieving your goals depends on several factors, including your background, determination, and most of all—your actions. No one can guarantee your success, but I can guarantee that if you don't take any action as a result of reading this book, you'll be as stuck as you are now.

However, if you are struggling with motivation as a result or part of a physical or mental health problem, please seek help from your healthcare provider first. You may still benefit from advice given in this book, once you've addressed any underlying problems, but please deal with your health appropriately.

So here is my plea to you: only read this book if you intend to take action.

Whether you're a middle-aged career-shifter trying to build enough motivation to make that jump, a student struggling to complete your college degree, a young mum trying to lose 'baby weight', or an employee dreaming of climbing the career ladder, you may find this book helpful.

But most of all, if you're disappointed with blanket, cure-all, 'motivational' quotes, apps, music/other magical devices, can't digest boring and heavy scientific reads, and are tired of 'get motivated' books, articles and posts—this is a must read for you.

Easy-to-read, concise, jam-packed with practical steps that can be adjusted to your specific situation - here is my system for you. Written to help you succeed - faster.

PART I

GETTING THE BASICS RIGHT

1

MOTIVATION - THEORY, 'TRUTHS', AND MYTHS

"*Horse is as everyone can see*" (1)

You knew this was coming, so let's deal with some theory before we jump into practice. I promise, it'll be short - only the stuff you need to know to understand motivation and use it to your advantage.

What is motivation?

According to Mullins (2), **motivation** is a '**driving force**' pushing **people** to **take action** to fulfil a **need**, uphold a **value** or achieve a **goal**.

Needs are physiological or emotional drivers, often very basic and required for survival, such as thirst, hunger, love or reproduction.

Values are higher-level drivers, representing ideas, principles, beliefs that are important to us, such as family, faith, well-being, or freedom.

Goals are outcomes towards which we work. We choose them consciously. Different people have different goals and these can change as they go through life.

Simply put, **motivation is the drive to meet a need or fill a void**, as basic as hunger or thirst, or more 'sophisticated'—such as the sense of belonging, or personal fulfilment.

Those motivation drivers can be grouped, according to their type, just like in Maslow's hierarchy of needs (see Fig 1).

Fig 1: Maslow's hierarchy of needs

According to Maslow the main needs that drive our behaviour form a pyramid with five levels:

1. Physiological needs - food, water, warmth, clothing, shelter
2. Safety needs - personal and financial security, health and well-being
3. Belongingness and love needs - social belonging, intimate relationships, family, friends
4. Esteem needs - self-esteem, respect, appreciation, feeling of accomplishment
5. Self-actualisation needs - achieving your full potential)

The first two levels are about basic needs, required for biological survival of our species. The next two meet our psychological needs, and the final one is about self-fulfilment.

As you can see in the figure, these levels form a pyramid with the most fundamental needs at the bottom, and higher-level needs towards the top.

We'll discuss the practical implications of Maslow's approach to motivation in chapters 3 and 5, but for now, I'd like go back to our **understanding of motivation.**

A few years ago, when I first started investigating the complex topic of human motivation, I realised that despite a great deal of research and academic discussion, the scholars are still **not clear how motivation actually works.**

We know it has something to do with our **biological instincts** (for instance, the one to pass on our genetic material). Motivation can **drive** us to **change our behaviour** (e.g. to go out to meet potential sexual partners to mate with to pass on our genes). But scientifically speaking, **our knowledge of what motivation is and how it works is still theoretical.**

Some of these theories are better supported by empirical data than others, but none seems able to clearly describe or explain what happens in all the cases.

Remember the horse from the quote at the opening of this chapter? I bet you wondered why I even put it there :-). This is how I see the current state of knowledge on human motivation: we sort of know what motivation looks like and what we can use it for, but we still struggle to describe it adequately, particularly in simple terms.

Bad news?

On the contrary. In practice, it means the hunch you have about that recently read book/article/lecture not really making you feel more motivated, is right. Even when a crowd around you is jumping up and down and shouting in unison with a Guru on the stage, you may not necessarily feel motivated to join in.

We are all different.

Strangely enough, even though in general, humans, like all living organisms, are motivated to pass on their genetic material in order for it to survive, some don't necessarily feel the urge to reproduce. This is a great example of how different people can be motivated by different values and goals.

And, as I've already mentioned, these values and goals are liable to change as we go through life.

Sadly, despite that, traditional approaches to boosting motivation don't seem to take these variations into consideration.

Let's looks at some widely popular 'truths' about motivation.

Motivational 'truths' and myths

Some people are motivated and some are not

It's easy to assume that those who watch TV or play games all day are unmotivated, and those who spend every morning in the gym or at their desks working on their books are.

Appearances can be deceptive.

So, what's at play here? Nothing more than individual differences in what different people feel motivated by. Some people want to pursue career success, wealth, health and fitness, and some simply enjoy a good game, a bit of daydreaming, or nice food more than anything else (3).

Motivation is an on-again off-again thing

This is another erroneous belief (3). Modern understanding of how motivation works sees this not as an issue of *when* you are motivated, but rather *what* your motivation is *focused on* at various points in your life.

As an example, let's consider the issue of food and the motivation to eat.

Sometimes you are hungry and motivated to eat. Sometimes you're not hungry and not motivated to eat. Sometimes you may not even be hungry, but motivated to eat, or hungry but not motivated to eat. Complicated, isn't it? But when you're not seeking food it doesn't mean you're not motivated to eat. The same happens with other goals. Your drive to seek success, happiness, freedom, etc. can vary in time and at different points in your life.

At this very moment in my life, I'm channelling all my internal drive into writing this book, because my daughter is away at her grandparents', and I have more time. But when she is back from her summer holidays, the focus of my motivation will change—I'll be spending more time with her and less on writing. Although I'll be as motivated to write as I was before, the focus of my motivation will be different.

The fact that you haven't reached your goals despite many attempts means you are not motivated enough to achieve them

This is my pet hate. I have been on the receiving end of this assumption many times.

'You haven't managed to cut down on carbohydrates you eat? You need to get motivated. You are not motivated enough to maintain a healthy diet.'

I heard this comment from a wellness coach while I was working on improving my nutrition. By the way, I wrote more about this experience in my book, *Hack Your Habits (4)*. When struggling with weight loss, I had faced a similar (and similarly wrong) assumption, in relation to sticking to a diet, maintaining regular exercise, or both.

I hate this assumption and not only because it blames the person for not wanting to achieve their goal enough. My main issue with this belief is its twisted logic. In my experience, the more times you have tried—despite all the failures—the more this is proof you are motivated to achieve this goal. So, your motivation might be spot on, but you've not discovered yet the correct method for using it.

Just imagine persisting for over twenty years, trying various strategies, failing, and starting all over again. And some people call this not being motivated enough?

C'mon! Stop listening to this BS.

You *are* motivated. The problem lies somewhere else, though. And this book will show you why this kind of negative thinking is a problem and, more importantly, how you can fix it.

If you're not working towards it now, you're not motivated to achieve it

There is an assumption that motivation activates your behaviour, pushing you to achieve your goals and persist at it. This is also called: the activating property of motivation and persistence in pursuing your goal (3).

While this is true to some extent, there are moments and situations in life, when inaction does not equal lack of motivation.

Here's an example.

A rabbit freezes when a predator is close. The rabbit may appear motionless and unmotivated to save its life, but inside, there is a hormonal storm, with adrenaline buzzing, preparing the animal to run for its life.

Conversely, if you aren't writing that book, or sweating out in the gym despite all your plans to do so, it doesn't mean you don't want to write or improve your fitness. It may simply mean that at this moment in your life you're focused on something else. And this is what happened to me when my daughter returned from her holidays. See how it works?

You have to be frantically wanting this 'like needing air' to be truly motivated

Have you ever heard that you will only be successful if you want to succeed as badly as you want to breathe?

Oh, yes, you need to want to achieve your goals in the first instance, but frantic pursuits of a goal don't necessarily equal powerful motivation. Just as going about it at a slower pace isn't a sign of being 'tepid' about your desire to succeed.

Vigour of responding to the stimulus, as it's formally known (3), may, of course, reflect the strength of your desire to achieve a particular goal (and the strength of your motivation). On the other hand, there are multiple factors at play. If a person is simply better at doing what the pursuit of their goal includes, they are more likely to engage in it with more energy.

When my daughter and I first started paper quilling (a form of art using strips of paper), getting the table ready, choosing the design and understanding how to make the necessary elements took us ages. We would whine a lot because the glue was temperamental, the elements too small, or our fingers were too clumsy. Everything took so much time and energy, whoever saw us do it, wondered if we enjoyed the activity at all.

Yes, we did. And yes, we were motivated to do it and to improve. But we had yet to develop the correct skills.

It's a totally different matter now.

These days, setting up the craft table and getting on with the new design takes only a few minutes. We can achieve more during our little sessions. We are more energetic. We don't complain about the difficulty level anymore. Do we look more motivated? You bet! Are we more motivated? Not really.

Next time you see or read about a rat, running around a maze looking for food faster than another rat, don't think it's more motivated to do it. It may be just better at navigating the maze than his less fortunate brother.

You can be motivated by other people

Have you ever met anyone who become inspired by someone else's deeds and wanted to follow in their footsteps and become an entrepreneur, a philanthropist, or a best-selling author?

We get inspired by stories of persistence, grit and success, or pep talks. But even though those beautiful and uplifting words can energise and push us to action, this is not always enough to keep us going. So, while someone's example may encourage you to *start* working on your first app, set up a non-profit organisation helping the less fortunate, or write your first book, it may not be enough to get you to achieve your goal.

The secret?

True motivation comes from within. You need to feel you really want it from the bottom of your heart.

There are many more examples, but I'll stop here. What I've just outlined are the false beliefs on motivation I've grappled with most. The idea that 'you need to get motivated' makes me want to grab the nearest heavy object and lob it through the nearest window.

OK, some of these approaches may work for some people, but assuming that if it's worked for them it must work for me, is wrong. I've met a lot of people, who were led to believe they were 'inadequately motivated' because they had failed to reach their goals time and again, despite all their efforts. As a result, these people were also disillusioned and discouraged by the accompanying reasoning that suggested their failure meant there was something wrong with their motivation and with themselves.

So, let me repeat it: if you've tried to achieve a goal, and failed multiple times, stop thinking you are not motivated enough! Don't try to 'get motivated' anymore. The likelihood is—**you *are* motivated.** Look at how much energy, time and often, money you have invested in reaching your goal. There is probably nothing wrong with your motivation, but there maybe something wrong with the way you're using it. You may need to use it differently. You may need to look at your goal and your drivers and redesign your goal-attainment strategy.

No worries, I'll help you do it. Just keep reading.

Having dealt with some of the motivational myths, in the next chapter we'll look at what works in the real world, and what might work for you.

2

WHAT SEEMS TO WORK

In the previous chapter, I talked about motivational misconceptions and what the current understanding of motivation is. In this chapter, I'll look more into the 'state of the knowledge' of what motivation is and how it works.

As I explained in Chapter 1, **motivation is a complex concept** and a lot of what we know about human behaviour drivers are theories—some of them more evidence-based than others. But this is a 'living, evolving knowledge', psychologists and other human behaviourists are still working on expanding their understanding of motivation.

Below, I've listed some of **the best understood and evidence-based approaches to motivation**. This is not a complete list, and yes—I have simplified a lot of things. If you want to explore this area in more depth, I'd encourage you to check the reference section.

But for those of you who just want 'the quick and dirty' on what seems to work for some of the people some of the time, here it is.

From what we know, motivation waxes and wanes throughout the day, and throughout our lives. It can be focused differently for different people and at different points in life. The energy associated with the motivated behaviour can also vary in intensity depending on many factors.

The importance of homeostasis and hedonism

One of my university friends was openly into 'energy preservation'. He would often just sleep, or lie on the sofa apparently doing nothing. When asked, he would say he was restoring his energy. He was also very good at avoiding problems. He would argue with people only when he considered the cause was worthy of defending. He always knew 'what was in it for him' and would carefully weigh the pros and cons of engaging in any activity. He told me that simply being happy and having peace and quiet was far too important for him to get worked up over what he considered 'inconsequential'.

Surprisingly to the people who thought he was lazy, he earned good grades and went onto becoming a fantastic doctor. When he worked, he worked really hard, but when he rested, well, he rested really hard. While I struggled to understand his apparent low activity at the time, now I can see this was a clever approach. I think he was a smart and very focused individual.

Over the years, I've met quite a few people who like the status quo, even though the reality may not be ideal. This is common in relationships in difficulties, with individuals who are not happy, but who keep on staying together, because upsetting the applecart would mean a lot of hassle and even more unhappiness.

Yes, wanting to have 'some peace and quiet', simply doing nothing, or energy conservation are quite common as motivators! So if you spend a lot of time on your sofa, it may be because you are motivated to do so and changing it would cost you too much.

The need for personal growth

Personal growth is a great motivator. Most of us aspire to something —whether bigger or smaller goals. Wanting to realise our full potential is one of the most important motivators specific only to our species.

The whole industry of self-improvement (self-help/personal development) has been built on it. This book is also written because humans seem to have a hardwired need to better themselves.

However, as I mentioned earlier, lower level needs, such as biological, or emotional, have to be met first ('most of the time') before we can attend to our self-actualisation, personal growth needs.

Classical conditioning

This is the 'Pavlov's dog' type of stimulus-response pairing. It relies on a connection created between stimulus in the environment and our response to it. A smell of your favourite food being cooked makes you think of the pleasure of eating it and it makes you feel happy. After a few repetitions, you'll start associating the smell with happiness. Although quite rudimentary, classical conditioning can also be used to motivate people.

Operant conditioning

This is a form of learning ('instrumental learning') where the behaviour is modified by the behaviour's consequences—be it a reward or a punishment. This approach has been quite popular in many settings.

I bet at least some of you experienced it during childhood, and maybe have used it with your own children. It is used in workplaces (productivity- and results-based bonuses, or penalties for not achieving targets), and many other settings. The idea is simple: to reinforce a desired behaviour and punish the undesired one. The reinforcement/punishment methodology, performed in various ways, has been shown to be effective to some extent (1).

Incentives

This approach is similar to operant conditioning. The principle is that incentives—such as rewards or punishment—generate emotions, and emotions drive human behaviours. Since people strive to reach goals that are emotionally meaningful and appealing to them (2), finding a goal that is emotionally appealing will motivate an individual to work towards it. In a nutshell, a goal becomes the incentive to work towards it.

The flip side of this approach is that if a goal, no matter how valid and laudable, is not emotionally appealing or meaningful to the individual, the motivation to achieve it will dissipate at some point.

This, in fact, is the premise of my approach to motivation. If it doesn't feed your soul, it won't work. So, no matter how socially laudable saving the planet is, or how much your parents want you to become a doctor, these motivators will not replace your own, deep and heartfelt desire.

Meaningful goals

Given what I wrote above regarding emotionally appealing incentives and goals, having **meaningful goals** is clearly an effective way to get and keep motivated. And conversely, it's hard to be motivated in an environment deprived of stimulus (goals). If you don't have goals that are important to you, it's hard to get or keep going.

Motivation is our ability to direct our behaviour towards or away from something, but we need a stimulus to which we respond. If you're hungry, your stimulus is your hunger. If you want to win that girl (or boy), your desire is what drives your motivation. If you want to achieve success in your career, this is what feeds your behaviour. But if you're not hungry, not interested in passing on your genes, or you have everything you can think of, there is nothing in your environment, internal or external, to make you get up and 'go and get it'.

Cognitive approaches to motivation, and self-determination theory

This group of strategies emphasise the importance of feeling competent and in control of your environment as a powerful motivator of human behaviour. There is a variety of terms used to describe those forces at play, however they seem to revolve around the following three drivers, based on the self-determination theory (2):

- **Competence (Mastery)**
- **Autonomy**
- **Relatedness**

According to the self-determination theory, these are 'hardwired' psychological needs, which have to be met for us to feel fulfilled and happy. If one of those needs is not adequately satisfied, the person intensifies their attempts to achieve the satisfaction. Sometimes however, if those attempts are thwarted, particularly, if the person doesn't feel in control of their situation, they may withdraw from the quest and 'give up' on their goal.

Throughout this book I will often refer to another set of terms that is very similar, but, in my opinion, more encompassing than the one above, based on Daniel Pink's excellent book, *Drive* (3):

- **Autonomy**

- Mastery
- Purpose

I prefer this distinction, because I believe **Purpose** is a broader concept. It encompasses relatedness to some extent, but takes it even further. In this instance, 'purpose' relates to working for a bigger goal that extends beyond just an individual's own immediate environment, to following the person's passion of serving others, and working on things that have potential to transform their world.

I also like Pink's approach to explaining intrinsic drivers because it can be directly applied to how many people choose to live and work these days.

These three motivational drivers are considered to be the intrinsic motivators (as opposed to extrinsic motivators) and I'll talk about it a little more in the next chapter.

WHAT YOU NEED TO KNOW

The purpose of this book is to provide you with easy-to-understand and useful information on motivation. Without getting into too much theoretical detail and without using difficult terminology, here is what I think is most important and most useful to know for the well informed, smart 'end user' (that is you) 😊.

1. You are motivated—sometimes to take action, sometimes to take no action

I'm sure you are aware our bodies and minds need rest from time to time. It's good to be active but it's good to take rest, too. Your motivation drives your behaviour according to your needs.

2. Your motivation can wax and wane over time

Yes, this is the way it is. Your motivation can be more or less strongly expressed. It depends on many factors, often on your environment, or on your current situation in life.

If you feel your motivation ebbs and flows, you're right. That's the way it is (1). You seem to have a lot of it when you first set a new goal. But motivation is an emotion and is capricious. There are so many reasons why this may be the way it is, but the bottom line is: your motivation will continue to fluctuate.

Let me stress it again: motivation comes and goes because that's in its nature. There is nothing wrong with you. And the best thing you can do is to accept it and change the way you use your motivation (I'll cover that later).

3. Relying on motivation to achieve your goals it is a bad idea

Because of what I said above, working towards a long-term goal using motivation is unsustainable. First of all, those moments of feeling 'pumped up' about your goal will come and go. Sometimes you will know why (e.g. you're coming down with a 'flu and you didn't sleep much last night and because of that you were late this morning, and your boss was unhappy with you, so going to the gym during your lunch break may be the last thing on your mind), but sometimes you won't.

The strength of your motivation will fluctuate, but if you truly want to achieve a goal, you need to have a steady approach to it. This book will show you how.

4. 'Getting motivated' is a waste of time and energy

Because your motivation fluctuates, and this may not be in your control, **using the precious time and energy you have on 'getting motivated' is not a smart approach**. Why? Because even if you do 'get motivated' today, you'll inevitably hit another low point some other day. On those days, it will feel as though you are swimming against the tide.

After the initial burst of energy to pursue your newly set goals, motivational low will come. This is natural (remember what I've said above?), and this is also the point when many people give up on their goals.

But if you're dedicated to your goals, you will push yourself harder, and try to 'motivate yourself' to carry on, even though your body is aching and your mind is numb.

Motivation is a source of energy; it charges your internal batteries. But the problem is, you don't really know how long it will last and when you will be able to charge your batteries again.

And if you had a battery like that feeding your vital organs, wouldn't you treat it carefully? Wouldn't you think twice before overtaxing it? Wouldn't you use it sparingly and consider the best way to use it, the best way to get most out of its limited life?

Fighting against a 'motivational low' by 'getting motivated' is not a very good use of the limited energy you have in your battery on that specific 'low power' day. Moreover, **draining your motivational resources will make you feel as though there is something wrong with your motivation, or worse—with you.** Many people struggle to carry on with the new behaviours after a while. Bad days, when you're tired, sleep-deprived, feeling down, or sick are bound to come. It's simply a fact of life.

People who are aware of the limits to their motivation and willpower don't waste their restricted supplies on 'getting motivated' or 'pushing on'. They use whatever energy and enthusiasm they have at the beginning to build smart systems instead. And those same smart systems allow them to carry on with their work when they're low on motivation or willpower.

As BJ Fogg, a behaviour design expert says, 'Motivation doesn't work. Systems do' (2). I write more about systems and how to build them in Chapter 13.

5. First things first

In Chapter 1 I talked about **Maslow's pyramid of needs**, which groups the main drivers of human behaviour into five levels. The bottom levels represent the most fundamental needs, required for our survival (such as food, water, rest, safe housing, financial security), and the higher-level needs belong to psychological (love, self-esteem) and self-fulfilment sphere. And as with any pyramid, in order to climb to the top, you need to get through the lower levels first.

In practice in means (3), that the **lower level needs have to be fulfilled at least to some extent most of the time before a higher-level need can be addressed.** It's hard to focus on self-development (self-actualisation) or other higher-level psychological needs if your lower level needs (physiological, safety, belongingness, self-esteem— so-called deprivation needs) aren't met. If you are hungry, thirsty, threatened with eviction, or feeling unloved and rejected, you will find it much harder to muster motivation to focus on fulfilling your passion for art, or pursuing happiness.

So, attend to your more pressing needs first, before embarking on self-development, and don't feel guilty or embarrassed about it. You cannot achieve much self-actualisation when your stomach is rumbling or you are feeling isolated and rejected.

6. You have motivation, but you may be using it incorrectly

Let me repeat it again: if you have tried many times to achieve a goal and failed, you have motivation to achieve this goal, but you have been probably using it incorrectly. Contrary to the popular belief, you don't have to 'motivate yourself' more. Instead, you need to look at the true nature of your motivation and the way you use it. This book will take you through the steps necessary to understand what your real motivational drivers are and how you can best put them to work so you can achieve your goals.

7. Being realistic about your goals is key to success

Following ambitious goals seems to result in considerable success professionally (3) and in greater life satisfaction/ happiness (4), but the effects are often short-lived, unless those goals are truly linked to what we care about.

To succeed in a long-haul pursuit, we also need to be realistic. Sadly, we humans tend to overestimate our competencies (5). As a result, we assume we'll be able to deal with whatever life throws at us, including obstacles on the way to achieving our goals. And the farther away the goal is, and the more we want it, the more likely we are to assume that the sheer desire of achieving that goal will suffice to overcome all obstacles.

The key to success when it comes to long-term goals is to understand that there will be obstacles and bad days on the journey, and to adjust the plan. People who use this method are much more likely to achieve their goals, than those who 'dream big', but are unrealistic.

The gist of my message here is: **if you want to achieve your long-term goal, you need to be realistic about it.** Envision potential obstacles to check if you're able to overcome them. If you do, go ahead, but if you don't feel you have what it takes, don't waste your energy and time chasing what's unrealistic.

8. Plan your goal achievement strategy on a bad, or an average day

I have an even bolder approach.

Ready?

I know how exhilarating it is to feel you want to pursue a goal. For me, I'm full of energy and enthusiasm. I feel I can move mountains. I can't wait to get started. This is a great feeling, but it can be as misleading as it is powerful.

Why?

As I said in the previous points, humans tend to overestimate our abilities and skills (remember all those talent show candidates that made you cringe?). Hence, **my counterintuitive but very effective response to this problem is not to jump to planning the goal-achieving journey on a 'pumped-up day'.** Instead, I wait until this energy settles. I wait until I feel 'normal' or flat again. Then I sit down to make the plan.

Because, when I feel 'pumped' and full of energy, I'm more likely to reach for the stars and assume I'll always feel the same way each day, while the reality is different.

However, if I plan my steps on a bad day, I'm more likely to plan for all those 'not-so-pumped' days. And if I can do it on a bad day, I know how much easier it is going to be on a day when I'm feeling energetic and enthusiastic again! Simple.

What I'm saying here is, if it works for me (and the clients I've helped over the years), it's likely to work for you too.

9. What motivates others doesn't have to motivate you

I've hinted at it before and will refer to it later, because this is a common problem underlying many people's struggles with motivation.

Have you ever felt inspired by other people's pursuits? I've been there, too.

Here's another of those little stories I promised not to add to illustrate my point.

When I was a student, I was impressed by the passion for mountaineering and trekking some of my friends had. I loved listening to their stories and looking at the photos they took of their adventures. Just imagine all those vast spaces, the beauty of your surroundings, the freedom, the wind in your hair, sleeping under the stars. I couldn't wait to go on a trip with them.

Luckily for me, and them, I started humbly, by doing a weekend trip into a mildly hilly area. Luckily, because I then discovered that being an introvert, I couldn't stand communal living and being surrounded by people all the time. Climbing was making me sick. My slow pace was annoying others, and I hate annoying others. And then came sleeping in a tent with millions of mosquitoes and other creatures which seemed to target only me. No, that was not for me, no matter how much I wanted to overcome it.

We are motivated only to pursue goals that are meaningful and emotionally appealing to us.

What appealed to me in the mountaineering and trekking were the opportunities to be close to the nature and admire its beauty. But while having close connections with others meant a lot to me too, the suffocating closeness and inability to escape it for safety reasons, didn't suit me at all.

10. If it doesn't feed your soul, it doesn't feed your soul

This is another lesson I've learnt from trying to do things that were not quite meaningful to me.

The biggest and the hardest truth I discovered was to realise that even though I had a job that most people generally considered as very fulfilling, well-respected, and overall rewarding, the rewards I was reaping were not aligned with what I found (and still find) rewarding. And no matter how much gratitude and praise, money, pride, success or admiration I was getting, my soul was starved. And in the end, I burnt out.

I bet you've heard this so many times, it may sound hollow, but it's true. You only have one life, so why waste it on pursuing the goals that don't really make you happy?

If it doesn't feed your soul, it doesn't feed your soul. Regardless of how big the reward you're getting is, if you don't care about it, you will feel unrewarded and deprived. You will crash and burn, just like I did.

II. Understand the difference between extrinsic and intrinsic motivation

Not all motivations are made equal. The first and most important difference is that there are **two major types of motivation: external (extrinsic)** and **internal (intrinsic)**. Understanding the differences between them is crucial to being and staying motivated throughout your life, whatever you do.

Extrinsic motivation is driven by external factors: your environment, your tasks, relationships with other people, etc. (6). To put it simply, extrinsic motivation is driven by **rewards**—whether material or not. Most often these are money, awards, accolades, etc. But it can also relate to things like being praised, respected, and appreciated. **Punishment and avoidance of punishment** are also powerful extrinsic drivers. This may take form of 'avoiding penalties' (e.g. for paying bills too late, or submitting your assignment after the deadline), or 'avoiding conflict' (e.g. keeping an important person happy or avoiding their anger).

Intrinsic (internal) **motivation**, on the other hand, comes from within. It's the desire to achieve enjoyment, fulfilment or simply experience fun/pleasure (7).

As I mentioned in the previous chapter, Daniel Pink (8) suggested, there are three main types of intrinsic drivers: **Mastery**, **Autonomy** and **Purpose**.

- **Autonomy** is the desire to direct your own life, be the master of your destiny and your own boss
- **Mastery** is about the urge to improve and develop yourself, your skills, your knowledge
- **Purpose** is about the need to do things for reasons other and bigger than yourself, helping others, building a better world

This **extrinsic/intrinsic difference** is crucial to understanding how to stay motivated, because these two types of motivation work in different ways and are useful for different kinds of goals. I will cover these issues in the book.

12. Intrinsic motivation drives our long-term goals

Don't get me wrong, both intrinsic and extrinsic motivations are important in life and goal achievement. They both have their upsides and downsides, but intrinsic motivation is the source of power for your long-term goals. Educational goals, career ambitions, artistic fulfilment or happiness cannot be achieved just by using 'carrots and sticks' or 'naming and shaming', or even monetary rewards.

If you really want to achieve one of those 'big goals', you need to explore what drives you intrinsically. And you need to be able to tap into that source of potent fuel.

If you don't know how to discover and navigate intrinsic motivation, don't worry, I'll explain it, step-by-step over the upcoming chapters.

Okay, I've just outlined **twelve key ideas**, it's a long list, I know. And although, it is not exhaustive, I have included the main points above. I hope it has helped you understand the key issues and principles necessary to take steps I will describe in this book.

Armed with this knowledge, I will now move onto exploring how to set up your motivation so it fuels your goals irrespective of motivational ups and downs, or life getting in your way. The focus of the next section of this book is getting your motivation right.

Turn the page to find out how to do it and let's get on with it.

PART II

GETTING YOUR MOTIVATION RIGHT

4

HOW TO MAKE SURE YOUR MOTIVATION ALWAYS WORKS FOR YOU

I f you've tried to achieve a goal and failed many times, you may have questioned your motivation, assuming it was insufficient.

In my experience, more often than not, this assumption is wrong.

Life gets in the way

Let's say you want to start working out regularly. You know that with a good exercise routine your physical and mental health will improve, you will sleep better, feel better, may even lose weight and improve your productivity. You need it all. So, you set yourself a goal of developing a daily exercise routine to be healthier and happier.

You do some research on suitable sports to take up and decide to join a local gym. You've got some workout gear at home, but since you haven't used it much in the past, you think you'd be more likely to exercise if you are held accountable by a personal trainer at the centre.

Together with the trainer, you decide that the best time to exercise is in the morning, so you start getting up earlier. You manage to do that for a few weeks. And then, you have an important morning meeting in town and skip a session. And then, you get sick. And then, winter comes in and it's harder to leave the house when it's cold and dark outside. So, you shift your training sessions to the evening. But evenings are even worse. All you want to do after a long day in the office is to get home, eat dinner, and relax in front of the TV.

I can totally relate to all this.

The most common and most ignored reason why we feel unmotivated

Yes, this may be just temporary 'downer' and in a week's time, or in spring you will feel motivated again. But perhaps your goal of taking up exercise to improve your well-being is not all that motivating for you?

Whoa! I know what you're thinking here, your thinking, 'C'mon, Joanna, who doesn't care about their wellbeing?'

Of course, you want to be healthier and happier!

I'm not questioning that. I'm not questioning your desire to exercise regularly. I'm questioning the way you understand not so much *what* you want, but *why* you want it.

One of the most common reasons people find themselves in situations where they 'run out of motivation' is that they embark on a long-term goal achievement journey for the wrong reason(s).

The best way to get your motivation right

A great number of questions I receive from my readers and people I work with, revolve around motivation. For many, their biggest challenge is identifying what drives them in life and then translating those drivers into the fuel for their goal-achievement plans. And that's why they find themselves in never-ending cycles of motivational 'highs and lows' and exhausting 'pump yourself up' sessions.

If you are one of those people, if you're sick and tired of having to motivate yourself constantly, here is something that can help.

Below is my **5-Step framework** that can help ensure that you have a powerful, lasting motivation for whatever goal you are working towards.

This **5-Step motivational framework** has helped me and many other people get the motivation 'right', discover what really matters, and use it to guide the goal-achievement plans without the exhausting cycle of having to 'get motivated'.

If you're looking for a strategy to help you make your dreams come true despite what life throws at you, this framework is for you.

5-Step Framework for Powerful, Lasting Motivation

Step 1. Identify what motivates you in life

Simple, isn't it? Just joking.

Unlike all those posts and eBooks telling you to just spend some time thinking about it, I'm not saying this is as simple as putting your mind to it.

Actually, I find that the mind—the rational side of us— often has little to do with it, and it's the heart—the emotional part of ourselves —that really matters here.

In my experience, **the biggest challenge to understanding personal drivers is to see beyond what we think we're driven by.** Over the years, with multiple commitments, life experience and various expectations, many of us lose sight of what is really important to us. It takes courage to even admit to ourselves that well, yes, our family/community/pursuit of freedom/career are important to us, but there is something much more powerful we're yearning for but feel too shy, embarrassed, or guilty to pursue.

Explore your true motivation not only with an open mind, but most importantly, with your *heart* open. Be brutally honest and gentle with yourself at the same time. Remember, nobody needs to know about it. You can keep it to yourself. But if you *are* able to discover what really motivates you and use it as a fuel to propel you towards your goals, you may be able to achieve the dreams you never thought possible.

I will explain how to discover what motivates you in life in Chapter 5.

Step 2. Align your goal with your motivation

It sounds obvious, but many people struggle with this step, too. Once you have a good understanding of what drives you in life, you can use this knowledge to ensure that the goal you have set for yourself is in line with it.

To use the example described earlier, if you're working on a fitness goal because you want to be healthier and happier, but you discover that you're a person who loves competing, or wants to become the best/the first/the only one, or maybe you simply enjoy learning—you have a problem.

Why? Because your competitive streak and the drive to become better at what you do is powered by the need to master, while health and well-being goals are (usually) not. Your goal (feeling better and happier) and your motivation (achievement, mastery) are misaligned.

You may be able to continue exercising for some time, particularly if you keep reminding yourself why good health and your happiness are important to you. You may even feel how exercise is improving your mental and physical health. But, there will still be something niggling you, a little discomfort, some weariness, maybe even disappointment. You will feel unfulfilled and may give up on exercising as a result. You might not admit it aloud, but inside, that little gremlin in your mind might be saying why bother since it's not bringing you what you want? Even if it sort-of does.

The route to success is often as simple as reframing your goal to match your motivation for it. If you can do this, most likely you will be able to pursue the same or a similar goal, but for a different reason. All it takes is admitting to yourself what you are driven by and rewording your goal to match it.

I explain how to align your goals with what drives you in life in Chapter 6.

Step 3. Match your goal to your motivation level

Yes, I know, the gurus have told you to go for gold, and 'commit 200%', because you're either in, fully committed, or out.

And in principle, I agree with them. I'm also an 'either all in or out' person. But, and there's always a little 'but' ...

As it's often is in life, we end up with multiple commitments and responsibilities. The longer you've lived, the more of those you are likely to have gathered.

So, consider how much motivation you have for a particular goal and adjust the size of it if necessary. This is a point where it's not helpful to be too bold, or too optimistic, thinking you'll find more motivation along the way.

Measure your motivation on an average day. Why? Because, as I mentioned earlier, when you are 'pumped up' and full of enthusiasm for your new goal, you're likely to assume this will last. And this is what you thought last time, and the time before, and last year too. And, by the way, did that work?

Well, you already have your answer.

My ability to achieve my long-term goals really shifted when I started matching my goals to the amount of motivation I had for that particular goal on an average day. If a goal I'm setting myself needs more energy than I have, I shrink the goal, or extend the time line. I want to write three books this year? Er, too ambitious, I don't have that much energy or time. How about one longer and one shorter book? Or, three full-length books in the next 18 months? These 'resized goals' may not look as well as the original ones, but I don't care. All I care about here is to have goals that I can actually achieve by working on them every day, regardless of my motivation level.

I explain how to match your goals with your motivation in Chapter 7.

Step 4. Reward yourself with what motivates you

To use a car and fuel analogy, sometimes, what you have in the tank is not enough to complete your journey. If your trip is really long, or you need to take a detour, or power up the heating or air-con, you'll use more fuel. You might even need more than your car's fuel tank can hold.

So, for those longer journeys, you may need to carry a jerrycan with you, or stop to fill your tank.

It's the same with long-term goals.

Here, I'm talking about **rewards**.

Rewards—whether little pleasures, big ticket items, or the simple sense of accomplishment—are great to keep you heading towards your goal, but only if you reward yourself with what matters to you. There is little use in trying to push yourself harder to prepare for an exam tomorrow with a promise of a chocolate bar if you don't like chocolate. It's the same as celebrating an achievement that doesn't really fill your heart with joy, is not motivational, and might actually be self-defeating.

Don't be afraid to use rewards to keep yourself going. Incentives such as money, praise, simple pleasures or avoidance of unpleasant consequences can be effective. Use them in challenging times, when you have a looming deadline, or you're going through a 'motivational low' and have to push through.

Just remember not to overuse those little rewards or their effectiveness will wear off.

I explain how to keep your motivation tank full in Chapter 7.

Step 5. Track your progress the right way

You can't really tell if you're getting closer to your goal, if you're not keeping an eye on your progress.

However, simply tracking your journey is not good enough, because if you track the wrong thing—an indicator that doesn't align with your motivation—you'll have a hard time sticking to your plan.

It's like wanting to become fitter to feel happier and tracking your weight, or your body fat percentage. Tracking metrics works best for Mastery-driven goals, and happiness is (usually) not one of them. To make sure your tracking system reflects your pursuit of happiness, you need to come up with a strategy to monitor how your fitness regime affects your happiness level. Similarly, if you're learning a foreign language to communicate with locals without a dictionary while on holidays, tracking the amount of time you spend revising the vocabulary is not a good system either. In this case, you would need a way to actually talk with native speakers and track your ability to communicate.

See?

I explain how to track your goals correctly in Chapter 9.

Whatever is fuelling your desire to achieve your goal, make sure it's reflected in your tracking method. This will not only ensure you know how far you have progressed, but it will also keep your motivation at the forefront of your mind. This, in turn, will top up your 'motivational tank.'

And that's it, that's **my formula for ensuring you have enough motivation to achieve your goals.**

Yes, it's that simple. Walk through the **5-Step Formula** and you won't give up during your next 'downer'. Once you've mastered the steps, you will be able to set your goals and achieve them, as planned.

But don't jump to the planning stage yet. Unless you are 100% clear on what really—and I mean *really*—motivates you in life, I advise you to keep reading. In the next chapter, I'll show you how to identify what motivates you in life.

5

WHAT'S YOUR FUEL? (IDENTIFY WHAT MOTIVATES YOU IN LIFE)

So, how do you discover what motivates you in life?

In the previous chapters I talked about the importance of understanding your motivation, but how on earth, do you discover what drives you in life?

As I said before, motivation is a complex area and there are still a lot of unknowns and uncertainties. We often don't really know how motivation and goal setting work, and even if we do know, there are always personal differences that further complicate things. In a nutshell: there is no simple answer, no one-size-fit-all, no 'best motivational strategy'.

Given the above, finding out what motivates you in life can be a complex process. But, to make it simpler for you, I suggest we focus on two approaches to motivation: Maslow's hierarchy of needs (1) and self-determination theory (2). I wrote about them in more detail in Chapter 2.

Why those two theories out of so many? Because in my experience, they make most sense and are easy to grasp from the practical, 'smart end user's' point of view.

So how should you approach the task of finding out what motivates you in life?

First things first

I mentioned before (Chapter 3) that it's hard to think about higher level needs, such as self-esteem or self-actualisation (which is where most self-improvement goals originate), if your basic needs aren't met. If you've ever been in a situation where the roof over your head was not secure (e.g. you were in rent arrears and threatened with eviction), you didn't have enough money to eat well, or were sick, you'll know how the stress resulting from those unmet needs can hijack any attempts at self-development.

I can relate to that, too. In my student times, and later, as a junior doctor, I often struggled with finances. I juggled my credit cards to pay my rent, or had to eat plain rice for breakfast, lunch and dinner. I worked odd jobs, extra hours and carried on giving private tuition on top of my regular student activities or work, to earn some money. Those financial worries played so much on my mind, I had trouble concentrating on my therapeutic work (my self- and professional development). No wonder, because from the Maslow's pyramid point of view, my needs were at the bottom levels–physiological and safety, while I was trying to fulfil my dream of self-actualisation.

If you are currently struggling to provide for those basic needs for yourself or your family, you are unlikely to feel motivated to work on self-improvement. And that's completely normal.

To be truly able to access higher-level motivators, you need to have your basic physiological, safety, and to some extent, your love and belonging, needs met.

But once you get to the point where you can start looking at having your sense of belonging, self-esteem, and particularly actualisation needs met, you can enter the realm of self-improvement.

We are talking intrinsic motivation, right?

As we discussed in the previous chapters, you know there is little point in setting off on a journey to long-term goals such as weight loss, writing a novel, or finishing that degree while relaying on extrinsic, 'carrot-and-sticks' type of motivation. So, if you really want to reach your destination, your motivational fuel needs to come from within you—it needs to be intrinsic.

Let's go over those three main intrinsic drivers again:

As I said before, I like Daniel Pink's take on the intrinsic motivation (3) with the distinction of: **Autonomy, Mastery,** and **Purpose.**

Autonomy is the desire to direct your own life, be the master of your destiny and your own boss. It's often related to the need to feel free from things like debt, bad health, unhappiness, and the pressure to conform.

Mastery relates to self-improvement, the urge to become better, faster, smarter. It's about learning to develop yourself, your skills, your knowledge. It's also often linked with the need for achievement and being 'the best', 'the first', or even 'the worst' (I know that's a bit weird, but technically, it does fit in with the picture).

Purpose is about the need to do things for reasons other and bigger than yourself, e.g. helping or serving others, building a better world, dedicating your life to looking after your family.

But what about extrinsic drivers?

If you find yourself being mostly driven by extrinsic rewards, such as money, praise, or the need for acceptance, it's likely that you have one or more unmet need from lower levels of Maslow's pyramid. You may be aware of that, or not. I encourage you to explore what's underneath it.

Being motivated by money or other money-like rewards is often linked to the need to provide for those basic needs. However, if your basic physiological needs are met and you're still chasing money, consider whether you have any gaps when it comes to your psychological needs. In my experience, people who are motivated by money but not for the reasons of survival, often do that because money serves as a proxy for power, accomplishment or as a boost to their self-esteem. These are all psychological needs, and a discussion on psychological needs falls beyond the scope of this book.

If you do things to please other people, to be praised, or avoid rejection, you're likely to have unmet needs in the emotional (psychological) sphere, and again, you are at one of the lower levels of Maslow's hierarchy.

These fundamental needs are important and cannot be dismissed. And, as I said before, you need to fill these gaps first before you can move onto exploring your intrinsic motivators.

How to identify what motivates you

Okay, enough theory, let's look at some practical exercises to help you discover what motivates you in life, so you can exploit it in your journey to ever-lasting motivation.

Answer the questions listed below with as much courage and honesty as you can. No one needs to know about it. This is an internal and a very personal exploration. You can write the answers down, or not. If you decide to commit them to paper or keyboard and screen, you can destroy it completely afterwards, or frame it and put it proudly on the wall. It's up to you. I'm not going to judge you. Your drivers and goals are none of my business. Just remember, stay safe, don't hurt anyone or yourself.

Here are the steps I suggest you follow:

1. Identify your most important needs

First of all, let's attend to those. You can use Maslow's pyramid of human needs (physiological, safety, love or belonging, esteem, and self-actualisation) to help.

- What do you need in order to feel happy?
- Are your basic needs such as food, shelter, and safety met?
- Are you pursuing self-actualisation?

2. Identify your values

The drive to live a life aligned with your values is a powerful motivator. Explore your values. Ask yourself the following questions (3):

- What is important to you? What do you value most in life?
- Think about what you really want out of life. What do you want your life to stand for? What do you want to do with your life?
- What sort of person do you want to be?
- What do you think your mission or purpose in this life is/are?

Also look at the following aspects of your life:

- What makes you happy and fulfilled?
- What do you truly enjoy doing?
- What would you do, even if no one paid you for it?
- What would you do if you had everything in life?

3. Explore what has driven your achievements so far

Look at your achievements so far, in areas of life important to you. What has helped you succeed? What did you think of or strive for when working towards your goal at the time? Why do you think you attained those goals?

Take your time when exploring your education, career, relationship successes. You can ask your nearest and dearest for their views, but be careful not to let other people's opinions influence you too much.

4. Put your findings into categories

Look at your answers to the above questions and fine-tune them. Try to think about your drivers in terms of extrinsic and intrinsic motivators. Assign them into the right categories.

Further define which of the types of extrinsic and/or intrinsic motivators your drivers belong to. Is it **rewards/punishment avoidance?** Is it **Autonomy, Mastery,** or **Purpose?**

It's likely that you're driven by more than one type of motivation. Most people can identify **some extrinsic and some intrinsic drivers.** When it comes to intrinsic motivators, you may have a clear favourite, or feel there is more than one thing that makes you tick. If so, you can list them in the order of how powerful they are.

You may end up with a number of motivators, belonging to different categories. Don't worry, it's ok. However, **try to identify at least one intrinsic motivator.**

If you end up with **more than one intrinsic motivator,** try to identify which of them you respond to most (**your strongest motivator**); or have an understanding which of your goals are motivated by what motivator(s).

5. Make sure it's your own motivation

I talk about personal motivators often in this book because, in my experience, this is one of the most common reasons why people 'run out of motivation' for their goals.

A great deal has been written about pursuing (or not) goals that other people may have for us. And many of you will be aware that sometimes we do follow our parents' dreams, work on what our bosses want us to do, or pursue our spouse's or family's idea of happiness.

What I'm getting at here is a different thing entirely. **Sometimes, people follow their own goals, for the reasons that come from other people, not their own hearts.**

As I said before, if it **doesn't feed your soul, it doesn't feed your soul.** Regardless of how big the reward you receive, if you are following your dreams for the reasons that don't resonate with you—i.e. if you don't care about your dreams—your rewards will be meaningless and you will feel unrewarded and deprived of motivation.

So, check whether the motivators you have identified come truly from you, from your dreams.

6. Test and tweak

As always, I encourage you to test your findings. You can set yourself a small goal and use the driver you think is your most powerful motivation. Observe, and note how well it works. Have you completed your goal quickly, without even feeling as though you were doing any real work? Did you feel energised, fulfilled, happy? Yes? Excellent, you've got it right. No? Not to worry, go through the exercise again, and test until you feel you've found the right method for you.

Discover what motivates you and use it wisely

I don't know about you, but discovering how motivation works was an eye-opener and the beginning of a new era for me. It was a painful discovery, but quite liberating. Without having the words to describe it, I always felt I needed to learn constantly and feel I was improving my knowledge, my skills, and my abilities. But for many years, I tried to be like other people. I tried to follow the passions other people suggested I might have. My parents insisted I sought financial stability, job security, and social conformity. Many of my friends at the time had inspiring visions of saving people's lives, or making money and seeking power.

I tried to fit in, while still searching for my passion and a sense of fulfillment. And while initially my academic and then clinical training pursuits provided me with multiple opportunities for learning and improvement, after I finally passed all my exams and became a specialist psychiatrist ('board certified', 'college fellow', or consultant psychiatrist), I started running out of avenues to explore. Yes, clinical knowledge is constantly expanding, but it's often just reiterations or expansions of existing knowledge. It wasn't challenging enough for me to feel I was really evolving. So, I continued telling myself lies about what drove me in life.

A couple of years ago, I reached the point where I realised I couldn't progress any further without a significant change in career trajectory. Since I didn't want to go into research, work for pharmaceutical companies, or continue in healthcare management, I decided to quit medicine completely to focus on other things.

As a result, I've set up my own business, became involved in a number of technology start-ups, trained as a teacher of ESOL (English for Speakers of Other Languages) and, most importantly, I finally got seriously into writing.

Despite the ongoing challenges, I am a much happier person now.

I'm slowly recovering from years of 'gratification starvation' and living incongruent to my values. I've achieved all that because I had the courage to be honest with myself and uncover my most powerful motivational driver in life and, more importantly, I found the courage to follow it.

I encourage you to explore what motivates you truly in life. It may be difficult and painful, it may take long, but it may give you access to a potent source of power to fuel your journeys to your dreams.

Action point:

To help you make the most of this book, I have created a workbook. If you don't have it yet, you can download it at: www.theshapeshifter-sclub.com/motivationworkbook. Use the Workbook as you go through this book to record your reflections and decision.

This chapter corresponds to Step 1 in Section I of the Workbook (page 3).

Answer the following questions and record your answers in the Workbook:

- What are my current most urgent needs (as per Maslow's hierarchy of needs)?

- What are my key values?

- What has driven me in life so far?

- What is (are) my main intrinsic motivational driver(s)?

6

WHERE DO YOU WANT TO GO? (ALIGN YOUR GOAL WITH YOUR MOTIVATION)

It may sound obvious, but I'll say it anyway: **motivation is useless if you don't have an outlet for it.**

Imagine having a powerful, beautiful car that can take you wherever you want to go, but not having anywhere to go. Even if it was driving for the pleasure of sitting behind the wheel of this fantastic machine, or showing off, you have a goal. But if you don't have a goal, or a destination, what's the point of having the car?

Some people set themselves goals because they are attracted by the payoffs. Some people set themselves goals because of the energy they feel inside. Often, it's hard to decide if you pursue a goal because you're motivated by it, or because you have motivation that aligns with it. It may be a bit of a 'chicken and egg' question, but whatever comes first, I suggest you make sure your goal aligns with your motivation.

In the previous chapter, we discussed the process of identifying what motivates you in life. Now, let's look at how to ensure your goal aligns with your motivation, in terms of direction and the amount of motivation required to attain it.

This step refers to goal-setting, but focuses only on a small part of it. Unfortunately, I'm unable to discuss the whole process of goal-setting because it's beyond the scope of this book.

In my experience, most people who complain of 'poor motivation' or of 'losing motivation', know what they want to achieve, or where they want to go, but fail to align their goals with their motivational drivers either in terms of direction, type, or amount.

To use the car metaphor again: these individuals have a destination, they have a car, but they don't have enough fuel to get there, or worse, they have the wrong type of fuel.

If this is the matter of the right type of fuel, but not enough fuel, they could probably limp along and arrive at their destination eventually, but imagine setting off on your journey in a diesel car with a tank full of petrol.

Yeah, they wouldn't get too far.

The same happens if you try to motivate yourself with things that don't resonate with you. Except maybe there is no risk of damage to your beautiful car.

So here is the key message for this chapter:

Match your goal to your motivation, not the other way around.

But what does it mean?

It means to:

- Make sure you're pursuing a goal fuelled by things that really matter to you, and to
- Match your goal to the amount of motivation you have to pursue it.

And this is how you can do it:

Let's say you want to lose weight. And you've discovered you are a person driven mainly by **Purpose**.

So, weight loss (expressed whatever way you wish to put it) is your goal and your motivation is serving people.

You have tried to lose weight many times in your life, to look better, to be healthier, and more recently, because your doctor told you that if you didn't lose weight you'd have some serious (insert as appropriate) health problems.

So, in order to protect your health, you embark on a weight loss program and you want to do it through exercise.

Sounds like you have a good motivation. After all, who doesn't care about their health?

We all do. Me too.

Except that, when I'm faced with a box of my favourite marshmallows, the thought of not wanting to risk my health might not be enough to stop me from eating what's not good for me.

A few years ago, I went through a stress-related rough patch. The symptoms were, chronic fatigue, poor memory and concentration, and falling productivity. As a result, I had problems doing my job, and since I was the sole breadwinner, our family was really struggling to make ends meet.

I was trying to manage the stress as much as I could, but my physical wellbeing was holding me back as well. I sought help from nutrition specialists and was told to change my diet, and specifically: to stop eating so many sweets and carbs, and stop eating so randomly.

You need to know that I have a sweet tooth and (sadly) had used food (and sweets in particular) as a stress-management strategy for many years. I'm a doctor, I knew it wasn't good for me, but I loved sweets and you know, when you're stressed, anything goes, really.

Having to cut down on sweets was my ultimate challenge. I was a veteran of sweet-elimination attempts. I knew what I should be eating and how. I knew it all, yet I still couldn't make it happen. I would maintain my good diet for a couple of days, and then slip back into the old pattern of munching my way through packets of biscuits and eating bread and jam as my main meal.

No, I'm not joking. I've been there far too many times. Those of you who are familiar with my *Hack Your Habits* book (1) would have heard this story, so treat it as a short refresher:

My health and my ability to function and provide for my family were deteriorating rapidly. Unsurprisingly, my wellness coach's frustration with me was growing.

He told me I had to motivate myself more. He reminded me of my health goals, of my family needing me. Of the old, super-effective self I wanted to return to. Of the long-desired weight loss. Ultimately, of my own survival. It doesn't really get much more powerful than that, does it?

All those really compelling goals, didn't I want to achieve them?

Of course, I did, but only until the next problem.

You see, no matter how laudable and important those goals sounded, they were framed (mainly) as Purpose- and Autonomy-driven goals. And that's not what lights my fire.

I was on the verge of dumping this whole 'wellness coaching' thing and just try more plodding on, while a crazy idea popped into my mind.

I shared my new approach with my coach - he did not sound impressed, but we agreed to give it a go.

It worked. Like a dream. Like nothing had ever worked before.

It was crazy, and ran against all the mainstream beliefs about motivation and goal-setting.

What did I do?

I simply aligned this goal of cutting down on carbs and sweets with my main motivational driver (Mastery, if you remember). I set myself a number of challenges revolving around the idea of resisting various sweet items in the cupboard, and beating my own 'records'. I supported it with a number of—even if I do say so myself—clever temptation-minimisation strategies and other tricks. All were aligned with my motivational drivers.

(You can read more about it, and my approach to habit hacking in my *Hack Your Habits* book:

In short, I recovered from that bad patch and I still use the same sweet-limiting strategies when I want to. I have even started to 'flirt' with intermittent fasting. Me, who couldn't live a day without any carbs! Of course, my habit hacking strategies helped enormously, but it all started with me having the courage to buck the established trends and align my goals with what truly lighted (and still lights) my fire.

How to align your goal with your motivational driver

As you can see in my example above, the 'alignment' may simply consist of you rewording the goal, but not the motivation! If you do this, you might need to amend your strategies, but more often than not, a simple 'exercise in semantics' can shift the process from a muddy track to a fast lane.

Your goal may remain the same, e.g. losing weight, cutting down on carbs, finishing your degree, having a better work-life balance, but you need to revisit the reason why you want to do it.

Below are the steps you may find helpful in ensuring your **goal is aligned with your motivation:**

Step 1. Find out what drives you in life

(As described in Chapter 4 - What's Your Fuel?)

Step 2. Identify why you want to achieve your goal

This is where you consider your motivation for pursuing this specific goal.

There are two main challenges here:

2a) Not seeing the wood for the trees

2b) Doing it for the wrong reason

Let's look at each of these points in detail

2a) Not seeing the wood for the trees

This type of problem is about having difficulty understanding your primary reason or reasons for wanting to achieve a particular goal. It could be because you're too busy to think about it properly, can't quite verbalise it, or have multiple reasons for wanting to achieve this individual goal.

The good news is, as long as you feel that the motivation for wanting to achieve this goal comes from your heart and you feel it strongly, you should be fine.

The (not so bad) news is that you may still need to do some work to uncover the real motivation. Don't settle for the first explanation that springs to your mind. Keep exploring until you're certain that the identified driver resonates with you. The ideal situation would be to have reached one (or more) of the three main intrinsic drivers (Mastery, Autonomy or Purpose), or one (or more) of the needs described in Maslow's pyramid of needs.

You can do it using a problem-solving technique called the **5 WHYs** (it's different from the my 5-Step Motivational Framework described in chapter 4), which consists of asking 'but why does it matter?' five times (see text Box below for an example).

Below is an example goal of having a better work-life balance analysed using the **5 WHYs technique**:

Q: Why do I want a better work-life balance?

A: Because my wife keeps telling me I work too much and don't spend enough time with her.

Q: But why does it matter?

A: Because I want her to stop nagging me, I'm tired of it.

Q: But why does it matter?

A: Because I'm tired of constant arguments at home.

Q: But why does it matter?

A: Because I don't want to argue with her. I love her.

Q: But why does it matter?

A: Because I love her I want her to be happy (OK-> this is **Purpose**, but let's do one more round just to make sure)

Q: But why does it matter?

A: Because my wife/my family is the most important element of my life? (Very strongly: **Purpose**-driven)

The **5-Whys technique** is a good approach, because the root cause is usually not identified until the fifth round. Alternatively, stop when you start circling around, or you start seeing the same answers. Be honest with yourself, and don't judge your motives. Put your 'explorer's hat' on and keep digging until you're satisfied with your findings.

2b) Doing it for the wrong reasons

This scenario, in my experience, is more difficult to manage. Technically speaking, you can go through the 5-Whys exercise described above, but in practice you need a good dose of honesty and courage.

This is often the case with people who have been told they should be doing this or that, going for gold, or chasing money, freedom etc. It was exactly my problem in the past, and I often come across people struggling with motivation for similar reasons.

In situations like this, I simply encourage people to explore their motivation with an open mind and an 'explorer's hat' on.

If this is your case, don't judge yourself, don't criticise your (or anyone else's) choices. Simply explore the 'why' behind your decision to pursue a specific goal.

And if you arrive at a conclusion that you're working towards your goal but for someone else's reason(s), you need to stop and consider what you want to do. Keep reading to find out how you can progress.

Step 3. Does your goal match your motivation?

Yes - Great! Go ahead with planning your goal-attainment strategy.

No? - Continue below.

Step 4. Revise/Reframe/Refrain

So, your goal and your motivation are misaligned?

No worries. Not all is lost. There are a number of things you can do to address this situation.

Typically, it is advised that you 'motivate yourself' for achieving a particular goal. Well, if there is a misalignment between your goal and your motivational drivers, you simply won't have enough fuel to power you to the end of your journey. This is why 'motivate yourself' strategy, in my experience, is pointless. It inevitably ends in a vicious cycle of motivational highs and lows and constant stop and start situation, which is inefficient and ineffective.

This is what I suggest you can do instead:

- **Revise your goal**

Revise your goal, not your motivation. I suggest you revisit what you really want out of the goal, and identify the aspects that most appeal to you on emotional level. Not intellectually, but emotionally. Again, it works best if it comes from your heart, not your head. Look specifically for things that resonate with your main motivational driver(s).

- **Reframe your goal**

If you find a strong emotional element in your goal, an element that aligns with your type of motivation, try to match the two.

For the 'work-life balance' person who is powered by Autonomy and craving time to himself, the goal of finishing work earlier to spend quality time with his wife, can shift its focus from **Purpose** to **Autonomy**, if it's reframed like this:

'I want to improve my work-life balance by finishing work earlier so I can walk home, instead of driving. This way I'll have time to myself and will get home less tired, and in a better mood'. This way, my interactions with my wife will be less tense/more relaxed.

I've jumped to some assumptions for this person's situation to simplify things, but hopefully you can see my reasoning behind it.

Make sure you know 'what's in it for you'

Whatever you're doing, make sure you know what's in it for you. It's great to be an altruist, but from the survival point of view, you also need to think of yourself. And let's be honest with ourselves, the harder the task, the more we need to feel there is a meaningful reward at the end of it.

So, if you're working on a goal not for yourself, but to keep someone else happy, reconsider 'what's in it for you'.

Even if you're the most altruistic individual on the planet, and all you want to do in life is to help other people and make them happy, I encourage you to bring it to the surface and embrace it as the driver for your goal.

- **Refrain from Pursuing** (at this moment in life)

Okay, but what about a situation where you cannot find enough excitement for a goal you've set to pursue? Maybe it's never been your goal, or maybe it all started off as your goal, but your priorities have changed since. The key message is that your goal is not aligned with your motivation and you cannot find anything in it for you.

Well, the reality is that situations like this happen. My approach to it would be to consider putting that particular goal on hold for now. Conserve your energy and spend it on something that matters more. But if, for whatever reason, you're unable to stop pursuing this goal, be aware that you're very likely to face more stop-start cycles, to need a lot of 'motivational strategies'. You're also likely to start feeling unfulfilled and exhausted.

I realise this is a long chapter, but hopefully you have a better understanding of how to ensure your goal and your motivation are well in line.

In the next chapter, I'll show you how you can make sure you have the right amount of motivation to achieve your goals.

Action point:

This chapter corresponds to Step 2 in Section I of the Workbook (page 4).

Answer the following and additional questions, and record your answers in the Workbook:

- What goal am I working on now?

- Why do I want to achieve it (what's my motivation for this goal)?

- Is it aligned with my main intrinsic motivational driver (see Step 1)

- If not:

  - Do I need to reframe it?
  - Do I need to revise it?
  - Do I need to refrain from pursuing this goal at this moment in my life?
  - When should I reconsider this goal?

MAKE SURE YOU HAVE THE RIGHT AMOUNT OF FUEL (MATCH YOUR GOAL TO THE AMOUNT OF MOTIVATION YOU HAVE)

In Chapter 5 (What's Your Fuel?) I offered a few ideas on how to discover what motivates you in life—your 'motivational fuel', so to speak. From the earlier chapters, you also know where you want to go, what goal(s) you want to achieve, and you are sure this aligns with your motivation. Now it's time to ensure you have enough motivation (fuel) to achieve this goal.

This is another point where my approach differs from the approaches suggested by the mainstream motivational experts.

In my experience, **the key to ensuring you have enough motivation to achieve your goal is to match your goal to your motivation level, not the other way around.**

What does this mean?

Imagine a situation where you set yourself a goal that exceeds your motivation for achieving it. Say, you decide to learn a foreign language in three months. Of course, you feel all excited about it at the beginning, but once the initial excitement wears off, two weeks into your course, you realise it's hard to keep going. You start skipping your lessons and you feel you've 'run out of motivation'.

A traditional approach to a situation like this is to 'pep up your motivation'. And a usual cycle of 'pumping yourself up' and 'running out of fuel' ensues.

My approach is different. First of all, I assume that life will get in the way. I also assume that unfortunately, it's not always 'mind over matter' and there are situations when my biggest dreams need go on the back burner until I can make them my priority again.

Sadly, many people do not pay enough attention to the fact that sometimes, 'shooting for the stars' is not going to work. Making your reward bigger, bolder, more appealing—to earn gazillions, climb Everest, or save lives, often falls flat when faced with the harsh realities of life.

How come?

If your goal is not immediately achievable, you face the problem of **delayed gratification**—putting off the reward until later (1). Delayed gratification is complicated by another cognitive bias, called **hyperbolic discounting** (2). Hyperbolic discounting is a belief that a smaller reward now (sleeping in) is worth more than a bigger reward later (learning a few new expressions this morning so you can increase your vocabulary, and be able to speak a foreign language in three months).

And then, of course, some of us have a tendency to maintain the status quo and conserve energy.

I know what I'm talking about in this respect. I have problems with delayed gratification myself. If I want something, I want it badly and I want it NOW. I am also rather lazy by nature. If it takes too much effort, I'm unlikely to do anything to attain it. Until recently, my strategies involved trying to pump myself up and remind myself of the rewards to come. But as you know, these strategies are not particularly effective.

This is why I've come up with the approach described below. The following six questions help me assess my goals against my current situation to make sure they are achievable and realistic at the given time, and within my context.

6 Questions to ask yourself to ensure your goal is achievable and realistic

Question 1: How much energy and time do you have at the moment?

Be honest with yourself here. Whether it's about a goal, or a strategy you've chosen to achieve your goal, look realistically at the amount of time and energy you have at this moment. Not tomorrow, or next week, but right now.

I want to specifically warn you against assuming that you will have more time next week, next month, or once you finish the latest big project, or after Christmas. Unless, you have hard evidence, backed by years of experience, (e.g. if you have school-age children and work from home, you're likely to be more productive during the school term), don't fall for this erroneous belief.

Question 2: What else do you need to change to achieve this specific goal?

This is one of the key questions many people ignore. Most of us find change difficult; some of us may even resist it. The more you need to change in your life to achieve your goal, the harder it will be to achieve. Think of all your current routines, quirks and habits. Do you need to change any of them? If so, how many? Would achieving this specific goal mean you had to start doing more of things you don't like, or conversely, less of something you enjoy doing? Is there anything you would have to learn to do in order to achieve this goal?

If you want to learn to speak a foreign language fluently so you can apply for the job of your dreams, you may think your motivation would be enough to 'power' you on your journey towards your goal. But do you have time to attend language classes twice a week, and spend thirty minutes every morning revising new vocabulary? Do you have to start getting up earlier, and you hate getting up earlier? Or maybe attending the evening classes means you have to give up your weekly night out with your friends? How can you get to the classes? Would you have to learn how to use the public transport, or drive through the heavy evening traffic and look for a parking space?

The more changes you have to make to achieve your goal, the more you need to learn, the more things you need to stop, or start doing, the greater the effort required to achieve your goal. And, the greater the effort you need to make, the smaller your chances of continuing with your plan. And this, as you can guess, lowers the possibility of a successful outcome.

Yes, I really mean it. Human nature is such that the majority tend to prefer the status quo, be it because of loss aversion, status quo bias, or preference for energy conservation (3). The result is that anything requiring effort is assessed and valued with regards to potential gains versus potential losses. The harder the journey to reach the reward, the bigger the reward needs to be. If the reward is not all that big or alluring, you'd better find an easy way to score it.

Question 3: How much time and energy can you dedicate to this goal?

As with question 1, you need to be cool-headed and honest with yourself when addressing this question. You should consider how much time and energy you can devote to this goal right now. Not next week, not once you've finished a particular work project, but right now. If you want to embark on a journey towards your goal once you've completed another project, then put the goal aside until that project is over. Because, between now and the point when you finished your project, a lot can happen in your life.

Look at your answer to Question 2 and consider if, **given the extent of the changes or adaptation required by this goal, you will still have time and energy to dedicate to your goal.** This is also when you need to consider all the other plans and projects you are working on in your life at the moment. Be particularly careful when considering **simultaneous goals.** Are they aligned, e.g. trying to lose weight and learning to cook healthy food? Will they 'compete' for your time and energy? Or maybe they are outright **conflicting** (e.g. trying to eat organic food and save money on food?).

Conversely, you may be pursuing **goals that reinforce each other,** such as wanting to eat healthily and trying to lose weight, or exercising regularly and improving your sleeping habits. In which case, you're in clover. Go for it.

Once you have a good sense of how much time and energy you are able to spend working on your current goal, move to the next question.

Question 4: Given the above, are you likely to achieve your goal as originally planned?

Do you really have enough time and energy to work on this goal? This appears to be a simple enough question to answer. There is a hidden 'but' though, and it often goes unnoticed, until you hit the wall and see it raising its ugly face again. The 'but' is, **delayed gratification.**

Yes, you need to take into consideration your ability to delay gratification when answering this question. This is when it often gets sticky for me, and it may for you if you suffer from '**instant gratification syndrome**'.

So, if you think you have enough time and energy to work on this goal right now, can you delay gratification until the goal is achieved?

If your answer is 'Yes', that's great news! Continue to Question 5.

However, **if your answer is 'No'**, consider the following questions:

- Can you drop any of the conflicting or competing projects?
- Do you need more time to achieve your goal?
- Do you need more energy to achieve your goal within allocated time?
- Do you need frequent smaller rewards?

Dropping a competing or even conflicting goal can give you that needed boost, so consider this in the first instance. Maybe, the only thing you have to do is to reduce the amount of change/adaptations required? You can also consider 'shrinking your goal' (making it less ambitious), or extending the time you give yourself to achieve it, or both.

If you **opt for a slower approach**, pay attention to possible **issues with even more delayed gratification** and put things in place to keep your motivation going (see Part III of the book for tips).

Continue until you have a resounding 'Yes'. If you are still struggling to reach a 'Yes', consider dropping or deferring this goal until your current situation changes.

Question 5: Is this goal appropriate in your current context?

This question is slightly different. So far, you've been considering whether attaining the goal is possible. **Some goals** or strategies may be **entirely possible**, achievable, implementable, but **it may not be the most appropriate thing to do.** For this question, you need to consider the potential **impact** your goal may have **on your social context.**

We all love to think that when it comes to pursuing our 'true dreams', we can ignore social conventions and obligations, shrug off what other people think of us, or even do without any social support at all. But the reality is often different. It's hard to give up your day job to concentrate on building a side business, if you have young children to support. It's also tough to take a gap year and travel and learn a language if your family/community expect you to settle down, find a job, get married etc. Sometimes, these are relatively minor yet still relevant issues, such as having to consider your co-workers when building a new productivity routine, or finding a way to exercise in a crowded flat.

Before you assume your goal is realistic and achievable, consider the impact of your decision to pursue this goal will have on your social context. Will your family approve of it? Will it affect your daily interactions with your flatmates or office mates? What about relationships with your friends, relations, colleagues, employers? Will following this plan mean you'll see less of them, or may not even be available to them as often as before? What will be the price you have to pay? Less emotional or even financial support from your parents? A breakup with your significant other? Less fun time with your friends? Reduced chances of promotion?

Given your answers, do you still think the goal is worth pursuing at this time and in this context? Are you prepared to pay the social price of pursuing it?

If your answers are still 'Yes', you really are onto a winner. But if any one of your answers is **'No', or 'Not quite'**, you may need to reconsider the issue. You may need to change either your goal, your strategy, or both.

And if this is the case with you, I suggest you **tweak your goal/strategy until you're satisfied with it** from the point of view of your current social context.

You can also decide to pursue your goal regardless of the identified issues. Ultimately, it's up to you. However, always think about the cost (in terms of time, effort, money) required to overcome/change/bypass the barrier(s) and difficulties you will encounter on your journey.

Once you're happy that your goal is realistic, achievable and implementable in your current context, proceed to Question 6.

Question 6: Do you accept this goal?

If you have no adjustments to make, then you're probably happy with your goal. However, if you've had to make some changes to your original plan, it may be a different story. That's why it's important to ask yourself if you still want to work towards this goal.

And if you don't feel compelled enough to pursue it, **consider the nearest best/acceptable option**. Again, ask yourself if you're happy with it. Rinse and repeat until you're satisfied with your new, revised goal. Alternatively, **consider abandoning the idea completely**, or **putting it on hold** until another time.

Don't be afraid to use this approach

So, this is my **6-Question approach to ensuring the goal I decide to pursue is realistic and achievable within my current reality.** I encourage you to go through the same steps, even though it may feel overwhelming.

Ever since I started adjusting my goals to match the amount of time and motivation I had at the time, as well as my social context, my ability to achieve has increased exponentially. I spent three years working on my first novel and it's still unfinished. I've never even started on many other book ideas. But my two non-fiction books were written and published in a matter of months! I wasted six years working towards a career pivot with a five-year detailed plan, close progress tracking and a coach to keep me accountable. But the revised, emergency plan took my reality into consideration, and got me out of my medical profession within two years.

It wasn't the lack of motivation that made me fail to achieve my goals for many years. It was the mismatch between my goal(s)/strategies and the amount of time and energy I had, my context and, most importantly, my misunderstanding of my main motivational driver.

Making sure the goal you choose to follow is realistic, achievable and appropriate is the key to success. Keep an eye on those aspects because, just as it happens in life, your circumstances may change and, with them, your context. Any changes in your context can have a huge impact on your goal. So, track your progress and, if at any point you realise you are not progressing enough, or have stopped completely, you may need to return to the **6-Questions** and consider your goal again.

This chapter is based largely on my habit-hacking strategy. If you would like to learn more about various aspects of your current context, and see how these and your personality may affect your ability to achieve behavioural change, check my book, _Hack Your Habits._

Action point:

This chapter corresponds to Step 3 in Section I of the Workbook (pages 5-6).

Answer the following and additional questions, and record your answers in the Workbook:

- How much energy and time do I have at the moment?

- How much time and energy can I dedicate to this goal?

- What else do I need to change to achieve this goal?

- Given the above, am I likely to achieve my goal as originally planned?

- Is this goal appropriate in my current context?

- Do I accept this goal?

PART III

KEEPING YOUR MOTIVATION

8

REWARD YOURSELF WITH WHAT MOTIVATES YOU

I've talked a lot about the importance of understanding what you are motivated by and aligning your goal with your motivation. Using the approach described in the previous chapters, will help you make sure you've got the correct type and amount of fuel into your motivational tank. And this usually should suffice to get you to your goal.

However, sometimes life gets in the way and we end up needing to 'top up the tank'. It's like with travelling by car, traffic jams, unexpected detours, heating or AC, lead to a heavier fuel use. Sometimes you need to stop and refuel your car. The same may happen with your 'motivational tank', and that's why you need to know **how you can reward yourself along the way to keep your motivation going.**

Be aware that motivation fluctuates

I've talked about it before in this book, so it shouldn't be a surprise. If you happen to have a bad day today, it doesn't mean it will be bad again tomorrow. Do as much as you can, using your systems, and see what happens tomorrow.

If it doesn't go away, remind yourself of what success means to you

Yes, no matter how altruistic you are, it always boils down to what's in it for you. Don't underestimate the importance of this message. Remind yourself why you're working towards a particular goal, and make sure your reward is expressed as a function of what drives you in life (see below).

Reward yourself with what matters to you

Obvious, isn't it? Sadly, many people try to reward themselves with things they don't care, or care little about.

I'm often guilty of misusing rewards and mistaking one thing for another. There were times when I was ashamed of what mattered to me, because it 'didn't look good enough', or was despised by other people. They were dark years of emotional starvation and doing a hell of a lot of hard work that didn't make me feel rewarded. As I mentioned earlier, it ended badly-with me burning out, although I have since recovered, and I will not make that mistake again.

I don't care what people think of my motivational drivers anymore. As long as it doesn't hurt anyone (it doesn't) or me (on the contrary - I'm happy again!), it's okay. Plus, I can put my work to good use and help others as a bonus.

If you are struggling with the clarity of what your reward may be, below are a few suggestions to check. As always, I encourage you to test and see what works for you.

- If you are driven mainly by **Autonomy**, you probably care a lot about your ability to direct your life, being in control of yourself, your life, your decisions, being your own boss. In practice, your goals are often driven by desire to work for yourself, live in a country that suits your needs, being financially, emotionally, legally, etc. independent from others or things (e.g. owning less, not being 'hooked on' anything).

- If you are driven mainly by **Mastery**, your reward is likely to be about: becoming better at something, building your competence, confidence, skills, overcoming your weaknesses or closing skill gaps. You are likely to be focused on the joy of learning, curiosity, discovering new things, creating beautiful things/machines/systems. There may be a 'competitive streak' to it as well, with you wanting to be the best/first/last person to achieve something.

- If you are a **Purpose**-driven person, your goals are likely to be about doing things for reasons other and bigger than yourself. In practice, this is often manifested by the desire to help or serve others, make the world a better place, contribute to society, leave a legacy. It can also be framed as 'paying back', doing good deeds, doing it for your family, or working towards becoming a better version of yourself. It can also be about finding your purpose in life.

A little note about purpose-driven goals and strategies

Self-help, or self-development goals, are often framed as purpose-driven goals. You need to be careful before assuming your goal is purpose-driven, because it may not be like that for you.

Purpose-fuelled motivational drivers are believed to be the most powerful and the most lasting, which is great, but they can also be a trap.

In my experience, this is the motivation most commonly given as a reason for seeking self-improvement. People often assume they are working on becoming better versions of themselves for purpose-related reasons because the self-improvement niche is geared that way, or because it's seen as the most noble way of being motivated. I want to warn you once again about not falling for this. Be honest about what drives you, however petty and little it may seem to others, or even yourself.

Your motivational drivers are what they are. I'm not saying you should drop Purpose-driven pursuits completely, if you're not motivated by Purpose. On the contrary. As I mentioned above, **Purpose** is the most powerful motivational driver. And I believe in doing things for others, serving others, helping the world to become a better place, contributing. This can and should be done **in addition** to being clear about what you find rewarding, and attending to your own emotional needs first.

Use extrinsic rewards wisely

I've spent most of the book telling you, that intrinsic motivation counts the most. And while this is true when it comes to long-distance goals, I don't want you to dismiss extrinsic motivation, and extrinsic rewards completely. Money and its equivalents, praise, avoidance of punishment or loss etc., can be very useful. So, let's now look at how you can use them wisely.

When you're really struggling to continue with your plan, (e.g. you hit a particularly boring or difficult point, or you're not feeling well but still have to carry on), consider using an extrinsic reward to top up your motivational tank.

Check Chapter 16 for tips on how to use extrinsic rewards.

Note: If you noticed you're 'hooked' on a particular reward (or behaviour) so much it takes over and you lose control, or if you experience any negative effect of your actions, seek appropriate help. Talk to your family doctor.

Warning: Motivation kills motivation

Have you ever heard of people who stopped enjoying their job once they started doing it for money? No, I'm not kidding, it's a real phenomenon, and psychologists even have a name for it—**motivation crowding theory** (1). Multiple studies show that rewarding people for things they enjoy doing, decreases the likelihood of people actually doing this thing. This is the strange reality of people who turn their hobbies into paid work.

This issue is particularly important when motivating others, but I've seen it at play when it comes to self-motivation. And if you're using rewards to boost your motivation, you need to be careful, too.

Hopefully, after reading this chapter, you have a better understanding of how you can use rewards to keep your motivation going even on a bad day.

Use what really appeals to you, test and change when necessary. And, don't overuse extrinsic rewards! In the next chapter, I'll show you another trick to help you keep that motivation tank topped up—smart progress tracking.

Action point:

This chapter corresponds to Step 4 in Section I of the Workbook (page 7).

Answer the following questions and record your answers in the Workbook:

- How can I keep my main intrinsic driver(s) at the forefront of my mind?

- What extrinsic rewards can I use to keep my motivation going?

9

TRACK YOUR PROGRESS THE RIGHT WAY

In the previous chapter, I covered a few 'keep it up' strategies to ensure your motivational tank is topped up while you're working towards your goal. In this chapter, I'll show you how you can make the most of goal tracking.

One of the key aspects of working toward your goals is tracking your progress. If you're working towards something, you'll often find it more efficient and motivational if you can measure your progress.

Obvious, isn't it?

The problem is, many people do it wrong, or fail to track their progress at all. And the price they pay is not only the risk of failing to achieve their goal, but also the risk of losing a great deal of motivational power along the way.

The key message for this chapter is:

A progress tracking system that is well-aligned with your motivational driver(s) not only keeps you on target, it also tops up your motivational tank. Conversely, a progress tracking strategy that is not aligned with your motivation can work against it.

Yes, you've heard me right. Something so apparently simple and obvious like **progress tracking** can affect your motivational resources.

How to track progress toward your goal

Your tracking strategy should make sense to you in the context of the goal you're pursuing. It should be aligned with your overall motivation for the goal and your main motivational driver. This way you're not only tracking progress, but also reinforcing motivation for continuing towards your goal.

Get the goal-motivation alignment right first

When choosing a progress tracking strategy, you need to take these two factors into consideration:

- **Your main motivational driver**

- **Your goal**

As you probably know by now, ideally, these two should be very closely aligned. If you're driven by **Autonomy** and working towards a goal of developing your writing career to quit your 9-to-5 job, and enjoy the freedom of not having a boss or office hours, this goal is well-aligned with your motivational driver.

If, however, you are driven by **Purpose** and working on your side business to quit your job and enjoy the freedoms of being independent, then you've got this wrong and you're likely to struggle.

For more tips on how to align your goal with your main motivational driver, go back to Chapter 6.

Design your tracking strategy

Once you are ensured your goal is aligned with your motivational driver, look at the outcome you are seeking and devise a way to track it.

Beware of tracking your progress by simply ticking off the steps completed. While this definitely works for some people and for some goals, it may completely flop for you.

The most common mistake people make when tracking their progress is to focus on metrics: money earned/saved, repetitions done, kilometres run, efficiency/effectiveness improved, etc. These metrics are focused on becoming faster, better, wealthier etc., and hence are **Mastery**-driven. They can work very well, but only for people who actually thrive on Mastery. If **Mastery** doesn't light *your* fire, this type of tracking is unlikely to make sense for you, and you'll struggle to care about those metrics.

To use the examples given above, if you're working on your side business so that you can quit your day job and become independent and you're driven by **Autonomy**, your progress tracking strategy should give you insight into how close you are to your goal of becoming independent.

But if you're working on your side business because you want to quit your job and focus on doing things that matter to you to fulfil your personal mission because you're driven by **Purpose**, then tracking how much closer you are to being independent will be useless. You need to focus on measuring a sense of how you're progressing towards working on stuff that matters to you.

A few suggestions on choosing your tracking strategy

I am often asked what and how to track goals.

The exact strategy will always depend on your specific situation, and I encourage you to test various approaches to make sure you find one that works for you.

Below are a few suggestions you may want to try.

- **Autonomy**

People driven by **Autonomy** may respond well to tracking things that reflect their **progress towards greater independence**—financially, physically, emotionally, etc. It may be something to do with achieving the state when they are able to quit your job, or climb the career ladder to a more independent, autonomous position. In personal life, it may be about them not having to live from payday to payday, or being able to afford hobbies they want to pursue.

Always refer back to *your* main motivational driver(s) and how you formulated your goal. If you are working to have a better life-work balance, so that you can pursue a hobby, track how much time you have managed to free up/spend doing stuff you want to do. If you're working on towards a more independent position, look at ways of tracking your progress to that professional independence.. This may mean tracking the number of meetings you've chaired, or independent field trips you have taken, rather than just marking your progress through salary scale.

- **Mastery**

People driven by **Mastery** usually like to **see their progress in all sorts of metrics.** They also like to see that they are improving and are better at a given task than they were yesterday, last week or last month, or being better than someone else, getting closer to their goal. This aligns quite well with the traditional strategies for progress tracking, i.e. writing down how many kilometres they run, checking in how their investment portfolio is doing, or even how many people read their social media posts.

Metrics are often pure joy for those driven by **Mastery**, and tracking is usually quite straightforward. So, if you are a Mastery-fuelled person, track whatever floats your boat: completed workout sessions, error-free repetitions, kilograms of body weight lost, money earned/saved.

• **Purpose**

People driven by **Purpose** will likely respond well to **tracking what** *reflects* **their Purpose,** whether it's doing things for others, serving, making the world a better place, or finding meaning in life.

For you, this may not be as straightforward as tracking money earned towards quitting your job or building your own business, or Mastery-inspired trackers, but you should try to frame the tracking activity in a way that measures your sense of purpose, fulfilment, meaning, etc. It may be, for instance, observing how your fitness routine improves your energy levels and gives you more strength to do charity work you want to do. Or, how your productivity routine frees up time you can spend on exploring your passion. Always try to find a close connection between your tracker and your goal.

In my experience, people driven by **Purpose** find tracking most frustrating, as traditionally, tracking takes into consideration things that are rooted in **Mastery** or even **Autonomy**. Very often, Purpose-driven goals are abandoned because tracking recommended by typical goal-attainment strategies doesn't make sense to people driven by **Purpose.**

Don't be discouraged though. Keep trying until you're satisfied that you've found a good indicator of your progress toward your goal. The closer, more direct the connection between the aspect you're tracking and the outcome you're seeking, the better. But if you're unable to find a direct link, use whatever tracker comes closest to what matters to you.

An exercise in semantics?

You may argue that this sort of 'exercise in semantics' is unnecessary, that it's just playing with words. And yes, it is right to some extent, but then again, semantics often matter. The way you frame your goal, or think about your strategy can help or hinder your progress. Out of those two scenarios, I recommend you go with something that can help you rather than not.

As always, I encourage you to test my suggestions. Try working towards your goal using whatever tracking method you have, and then switch to a new tracking method to see if it makes a difference to the level of motivation you have for you goal.

In the next chapters, I'll talk more about the pitfalls of getting motivation wrong. Keep reading to make sure you don't make those mistakes!

Action point:

This chapter corresponds to Step 5 In Section 1 of the Workbook (page 7).

Answer the following questions and record your answers in the Workbook:

- What outcomes can I track to ensure I'm progressing towards my goal?

- What metrics/indicators of progress can I track? How am I going to record my progress?

10

SEVEN (SURPRISING) REASONS WHY PEOPLE LOSE MOTIVATION SO QUICKLY

This chapter was originally published on EverydayPowerBlog.com - it has been adapted and updated for the purpose of this book

It's frustrating, isn't it? You're crystal-clear on what you want to achieve. You have a detailed action plan. You have enough motivation to get there. You want to be happy and healthy. You want a fulfilling career, a purposeful, balanced life.

So why, the heck, don't you feel like pursuing your goals anymore?

Why did you skip the gym session this morning and eat junk food instead of the healthy salad? Why did you say yes to another project even though you swore not to take on any more work?

Why did you waste time mindlessly browsing the Net instead of working on your business idea?

Of course, you still want to be healthier, happier and all that, but you are tired of having to constantly 'motivate yourself' and find ways to boost your willpower to keep going.

So why did your motivation fail you?

You're wondering if there is anything wrong with it.

You fear there may be something wrong with you.

Stop beating yourself up about your disappearing or dwindling motivation. The reason why you've lost it so quickly may be surprising and easier to fix than trying to constantly 'motivate yourself'.

Here are seven reasons why you may lose motivation quickly:

1. Because it is so

Psychologists have studied motivational ebbs and flows for years. Conclusions? Motivation is a dynamic process that fluctuates throughout the day, the week, and throughout life (1). There are many complex reasons why it happens, and we may not have influence over some, if any of them.

But it's not all bad news.

If your motivation is low now, it means it may get better at some point, whether or not you do anything about it.

The key issue is not to rely on motivation. Yes, motivation is important in the overall direction- and goal-setting for your life, career, your business, but don't depend on it in your day-to-day struggles. Create routines and systems to carry you through the ups and downs instead, (check Chapter 13 on how to do it).

2. Because you're tired or hungry

Yes, really!

If the goals you're pursuing require you to control your natural impulses (such as to eat chocolate, be lazy, or spend money), or stop you making multiple decisions (e.g. tasks to prioritise, projects to take on, healthy eating options), you're likely to need a lot of willpower to carry on. And if you use your willpower, you're at risk of **willpower/ego depletion** (2) at some point.

Ego depletion theory suggests that when you're tired of constantly controlling your behaviour, suppressing your impulses and making decisions, your ability to resist temptations falls away. Seems logical, yes?

According to Baumeister and his colleagues (3), your motivation will suffer if your willpower (ego) tank is low. Apparently, low glucose diminishes the ability to self-control and push on in the face of difficult choices.

So, if you want to keep working towards you goal, even on a bad day, make sure you use your willpower wisely (prioritise the tasks you need it for!), allow it to recover (rest and restoration!), and take care of your glucose levels (choose a healthy and balanced diet).

3. You rely on one type of motivation

As I mentioned earlier, there are **two types of motivation: intrinsic** (internal, from within you) and **extrinsic** (external, from outside you).

You may remember these types of motivation differ in many ways and can serve different purposes.

Extrinsic motivation may work very well, but only for short periods. That's why the vision of yet another pay rise may not be enough for you to improve your performance. Students commonly struggle with it. Yes, good grades are great and keep your parents happy, but if you're only studying to keep your parents happy and graduate with accolades, gratification is unlikely to last too long, and at some point, you'll notice you don't care about it anymore.

Intrinsic motivation is what drives people through life, providing meaning and purpose. Intrinsic motivation is essential to achieving long-term goals.

That's right. However, simply relying on your higher drivers may not be enough. Sometimes when the going gets tough, when you feel like you're wading through mud, there is no inspirational quote that can lift you up from that motivational low. Yet, you still need to keep up and deliver on time, to spec, and within budget.

Both types of motivation have their roles to play. If you want to achieve your goals, you shouldn't rely on just one type of motivational driver. Extrinsic motivation will peter out eventually. Your intrinsic motivation will go through highs and lows.

The best way to avoid losing your motivation quickly is to make sure you have a mix of drivers to power you on your journey.

4. Because your motivation is out of balance

I've mentioned above that fuelling your motivational tank with only one type of motivation is likely to lead to a goal-achievement failure, but so is getting the mix wrong.

To achieve your goals, particularly longer-term, more complex ones (e.g. developing healthy habits, building a successful business, completing a university degree), you need a mix of **intrinsic** and **extrinsic** drivers, and you need to use them at the right moments.

Intrinsic motivation is great for creating a vision and setting long-term goals. It will last long and drive you through life.

Extrinsic rewards will help you kick-start the change (e.g. to start following your exercise routine, or avoiding distractions at work). It will also give you that well-needed boost before the deadline (avoid punishment), or when you are bogged down with details.

Use each of them wisely and carefully. Don't overdo extrinsic drivers, and keep your aspirational, internal motives fresh in your mind.

5. Because you're following the wrong goals

I've said this many times in this book: whether you're trying to make someone else's dreams come true, or just spending time and effort on things that don't truly matter to you, your motivation will inevitably peter out. If you haven't invested in pursuing your goals (or are only pretending to do so), you are unlikely to succeed.

So, when you feel you can't keep chasing that promotion, better grades, or independent lifestyle, stop and ask yourself: Do I really care? Is this my goal? Is this the right time to pursue it? Do I truly want to invest time and effort into accomplishing it?

6. Because your life circumstances have changed

Seven years ago, I made a decision to change careers. I had a clear plan: step-by-step, with milestones and metrics and powerful motivation. I set off on my journey, measuring my progress. I achieved some milestones, just as planned. Great.

And then, four years into my five-year plan, somehow my progress slowed down. I could not get pass a certain stage. I felt like I was **banging my head against a brick wall.** I tried all the regular tricks: boosting my motivation, thinking about a better future, I even had an accountability coach! But still little happened.

It didn't occur to me until a year later. While I was toiling away making my dream plan come true, that my life had changed. *I had changed.* My priorities had changed. I ended up reassessing my goals and my motivation for achieving them. Now, eighteen months into my new life and new pursuits, I'm happily working towards a different set of goals. Full steam ahead!

If you feel your motivation for pursuing your dreams has softened and you don't feel so strongly about it anymore, reassess your path. Look at your goals and your drivers. Are they still relevant to you? Do they still fit in with your life?

7. Because you put the wrong fuel in the tank

I've left this one for dessert. This is my newest discovery and a very powerful one. It took me at least twenty years to arrive at it.

But it's not uncommon. Over the past couple of years, I've spoken to a number of people who got stuck in a similar trap: travelling to their chosen destinations with the wrong fuel in their tank.

I'm a bit cryptic, I know. Here is what I mean.

Motivation is the fuel that powers our mental engines to pursue our goals. And just like with real fuel and cars, some of us run different types of 'motivational fuel' than others.

You know the difference between extrinsic and intrinsic motivation already (see point 3) and you are aware you need a good balance between them (point 4). But even with the good mix of intrinsic and extrinsic motivators, you can still get it wrong.

Apply the wrong kind of intrinsic motivation to your goals, and just like with putting petrol (gasoline) into a diesel car, you won't get too far, and your engine won't thank you either.

If you need to have a higher purpose in life, pursuing a goal that emphasises mastery will not make you feel fulfilled. If you love self-improvement for the fun of it, chasing financial independence will do little to improve your motivation.

The bottom line is remaining true to yourself. Understand what drives you and be honest with yourself.

Your motivation to pursue even the biggest and most powerful of your goals will wax and wane as you continue through your journey. Managing those situations is easier when you understand the reason why it's happening. With better understanding of what's going on you can prepare yourself better for those moments, or prevent them from happening in the first place.

Now, you know what may be causing your motivational low, next time you feel you can't whip up any more enthusiasm for that work-out, or can't say no to the wrong project, or simply don't have the strength to decline another slice of cake, pause to reflect on what may be going on. Once you are clear, apply the appropriate strategy and see if it helps.

Don't give up! Your ultimate goal, your success, is awaiting.

11

KEY CHALLENGES AND HOW TO DEAL
WITH THEM

I n this chapter, I'll look at four key motivational challenges
you're likely to come across when working towards your goals,
particularly if these are long-term goals.

These issues are common, and they arise from the nature of motivation itself, as well as your specific situation. In a way, these are issues
to be aware of and not to fight against.

I. Getting your hierarchy of needs wrong

I talked about this in more detail in Chapters I and 3, so I only briefly
remind you that Maslow's hierarchy of needs is a theory that looks at
our motivational drivers from the point of view of various levels of
needs.

At the very bottom, we have physiological needs, such as hunger,
thirst or sex. You have probably experienced it. When you're hungry,
thirsty, or full of sexual tension, it's difficult to focus on anything else,
no matter how important. Only once these basic needs are met, we
can move onto the 'higher levels'.

The same is true for our safety or psychological needs—unless these are met and we feel safe, loved and respected, it's hard to work on self-actualisation.

As most self-development goals belong to the self-actualisation level in the pyramid, before you can successfully focus on those, you need to make sure that the other, lower-level needs are also met. The key to success is to realise what you are currently driven by and don't push it beyond what's possible at that moment.

If you're working on your career goals to earn enough to move to a safer home, your motivation is located at the safety level. And that's absolutely fine. Stay aware of it, and make sure this need is met first, before embarking on a mission to feel fulfilled in your job because, if that is the case, the latter goal is unlikely to be achieved.

How to deal with this challenge:

The bottom line is this. As long as you understand where you're starting from, and as long as you don't harm yourself or anyone else, and you feel strongly connected to your motivation, it doesn't really matter what drives your behaviour. Be aware where you are and keep working towards your goal. Once your lower level needs are met, you can look at a higher-level goal. If you try to skip a level, without making sure your other, more basic needs are being met, you are likely to fail to achieve your goal.

If you notice that you're struggling to achieve a higher-level, self-actualisation goal, ask yourself if your other needs have been adequately met. If not, consider how you can attend to them first.

2. Everything changes, including your motivation

As I mentioned above, you should attend to your lower level needs first before embarking on a self-actualisation adventure. Be aware that needs and motivational drivers and their importance to you change throughout your lives. When your children are young, your physiological and safety needs may come forward. But once your kids have left the nest, you may not need such a big house, or can move to a less expensive catchment area as you don't need to worry about school zones anymore. Conversely, if you're working towards a self-actualisation goal and start having health problems, your self-actualisation goal will likely lose importance in favour of physiological or safety needs. Once you feel better, your needs will change as well.

How to deal with this challenge:

Whether in the process of natural processes in life or through accidents/incidents, your needs and motivation that derive from them are likely to change over time. Some drivers will stop being important or relevant, and other will rise. Be aware of this situation and keep an eye on your changing inner and outer environment.

3. Your limitations and constraints affect your motivation

Sadly, however much I'd love to tell you that you're totally in control of your life, (and how much I'd love to believe I'm totally in control of *my* life), this is not always the case. For a variety of reasons, we are not always free to do what we choose, because this may harm or negatively affect others, or because there are other things in our lives that are more important/more urgent at any given time.

As I said before, life sometimes gets in the way. There are moments in life, when you don't have a choice but to focus on caring for a sick family member, or dealing with an imminent layoff, rather than climbing the career ladder, or seeking spiritual fulfilment.

Life is likely to throw a curve ball at you from time to time, and it's important to understand and accept it. You also need to be able to recognise the limitations (what's possible) and constraints (what's appropriate) you have in life, and how they affect your ability to work toward your goal.

If you find yourself unable to progress towards your goal, having to constantly reprioritise it, maybe even feeling that 'the world is against you', check if you have not, in fact, encountered a limitation or a constraint.

Most often, **limitations and constraints** will be **imposed** by **your environment**, and could be:

- **Physical** - e.g. unsafe neighbourhood, lack of money, low-paid job
- **Emotional** - e.g. dealing with a stressful event, or
- **Social** – e.g. your family, your boss, the rights and needs of other people.

Sometimes, limitations or constraints will come from within you, and may be your unmet need of being loved or feeling appreciated, or the emotional aftermath of a relationship breakdown.

How to deal with this challenge:

Constraints and limitations are often socially or culturally mediated. If you belong to a particular social unit, (be it your family, a group of friends, a church, a profession, etc.), you may need to conform to the rules imposed by the group. For instance: you might have to pause your career because it is culturally/socially required that you look after your ailing parents or your children, or you may choose to stay in a job you hate because your family needs a regular income.

You may take on this duty happily, or feel forced to do it. It may be driven by your need to belong, be loved, or be worthy. Whatever it is, this is part of your current context (at that time), and I recommend you not to judge it. Choices we make are influenced by a variety of factors and only you are able to fully appreciate your current situation.

Make your choice and stay aware of the origins of your motivation. Accept the fact that at times, it may not be appropriate to pursue a specific goal because of your social or cultural obligations, even though it's perfectly possible and achievable. Put that pursuit of happiness, or creative endeavours on hold until your situation changes.

4. Problems with delayed gratification

I admit, this one is a real problem for me and many of my clients. Delayed or deferred gratification is a reward put off until later. And the ability to resist temptation to get it now, in favour of a (usually greater) reward later, is one of the strongest predictors of success (1). Forty years of research clearly indicates that the better you are at controlling your impulses and resisting the temptation of attaining this reward now (immediate gratification), the more likely you are to achieve success in the future.

Why? Because most of our pursuits are long-term goals with delayed rewards. Education, career success, fulfilling relationship with others, happiness, none of these attainments happen overnight. Many of these endeavours take years of self-denial, sacrifice, and, indeed, delayed gratification.

However, if you, like me, have to live with what Tim Urban calls an 'Instant Gratification Monkey' in your brain (2), you may need to take a different approach to it.

'Instant Gratification Monkey' Problem?

How do you know if you have this problem? Many people I've talked to are aware of it to a greater or lesser extent. The most common manifestation of an instant gratification challenge is being distracted by things that look more interesting, or are just new, pretty, more exciting, when you're supposed to be working on a long-term project. Looking for 'mood boosters' such as funny videos or pictures (I admit, this is one of my weaknesses), while working on something long term may also be the sign.

Many of my fellow authors admit they check their book sale reports several times per day, often because they need a reinforcement that people are in fact buying, reading and enjoying their books.

How to deal with this challenge:

The traditional approach is to keep reminding yourself of the bigger reward to come. And if it works for you, great, do it. You may want to create a vision board, or write your reward in bold and put it up on the wall, or have it as your screensaver.

You can start practising delayed gratification with simple self-restraint exercises, such as putting off something enjoyable, or using willpower to stop yourself from following an impulse, even if only for a few minutes. Apparently, studies show (3) that even those simple activities can strengthen your ability to defer gratification.

But if you have tried these strategies and they haven't been effective (enough), you may need to be more creative and even (oh, the horror!), do something forbidden by mainstream motivational 'gurus', and satisfy your need for instant rewards.

For me, the best solution is to simultaneously: keep my 'instant gratification monkey' happy, and keep progressing towards my goals.

Here is how I deal with my 'Instant Gratification Monkey'

I break tasks into manageable chunks and pepper them with rewards

I break the long-term goal into key milestones and steps. Then, I create micro-rewards to give myself along the way, each time I complete a step or achieve a milestone. In practice, it often involves a number of very short breaks, no longer than a few seconds. I simply check my book stats, or emails, or walk to the kitchen and back. It is important to note that I do not open any emails/messages, I don't get involved in any conversation, but I just allow myself a few moments to break the routine.

Sometimes, on a really bad day, or while working on a particularly challenging project (such as editing this chapter), I can't manage more than a few minutes of sustained work at a time. I know, it's not much, but that's ok as long as I keep the breaks really short (under a minute). After all, I can achieve much more in those five minute bursts of activity than if I wasn't doing anything at all.

Novelty, change of scenery, a quick mood buster (a.k.a. a funny cat video), can help me to keep going. Once my 'Instant Gratification Monkey' is fed and happy, I can return to my main task with renewed vigour.

I build systems to outsmart my natural laziness and my Instant Gratification Monkey

This is my biggest 'secret to success'. When I feel motivated and 'pumped' about a new goal, I use this energy to create a system that will keep me working on the goal before my natural laziness kicks in. I also take my issue with delayed gratification into consideration by building in mechanisms that do not allow me to indulge in those activities for longer than a few seconds.

My systems are based on my weaknesses, previous failures, and I generally assume the worst-case scenario. I often go with the line of least resistance and make the task so easy I cannot fail at it. I also create default options, so I don't have any other choices but to proceed with the one I've 'pre-programmed'. It may be something as simple as choosing the easiest type of exercise to do, or having only healthy snacks available in the house. This way, I make myself do what I should be doing (e.g. exercising, limiting sweet snacks) even when I feel unmotivated, tired and super-lazy.

Note: If you choose to follow my example and 'feed your Instant Gratification Monkey', I suggest you build those systems first. These systems work on the basis of habit formation (temptation limitation or resistance boosters) and you can read more about them in my book, *Hack Your Habits (4)*.

In this chapter, I presented the most common challenges that are likely to affect your motivation throughout your life. Be aware of them, accept you don't always have full control over your life, and deal with what you can address. Honestly, if you're hungry, over-worked or under a lot of stress, working on a higher-lever goal may not be realistic. Attend to your more basic needs first before embarking on a self-actualisation adventure. Sometimes, it's better to wait until the time is right.

Action point:

This chapter corresponds to Section II of the Workbook (page 8).

Answer the following questions and record your answers in the Workbook:

- What are potential problems I may encounter while working on this goal?

- What can I do to counteract/minimise their impact on my motivation?

THE GREAT MOTIVATIONAL HOAX - WHY SETTING POWERFUL GOALS CAN GET YOU NOWHERE

This chapter was originally written as a blog post. It has been adapted for the purposes of this book.

You've been pouring your heart and soul into your goals. You've read all that's out there about goal setting. You've made your goals SMART. You visualise them regularly. You have a strong motivation, and you're clear on your 'why'.

You constantly fight off temptations and distractions, focusing on the future payoff.

You've invested in goal-tracking apps, books, and courses, but ... you never seem to be able to achieve your goals.

Of course, you want that work promotion ... start your own business ... lose weight ... finish that book, but somehow your motivation always fails you.

No matter how much you try to 'motivate yourself,' how many inspirational posts you read, or how much you visualise your success, at some point you run out of the energy needed to carry on. You're too tired, too busy, or you just stop caring.

Your motivation has withered and failed you.

But you really do want to lose that weight, make that career move, publish your novel.

So, you start all over. You set your goals, galvanise yourself, remind yourself of your 'why' ...

And it works, until it stops working—again.

And you're back to square one.

The most frustrating thing about motivation

Motivational battles can be exhausting and disheartening, but it's not even your lack of progress that's most discouraging.

It's the fact that going through this vicious cycle of motivational ups and downs makes you feel like a failure, like someone who will never be able to achieve any success in life.

Why trying harder is not always your best solution

So, you search for better solutions to your failing motivation. You listen to goal-setting experts and motivational speakers who tell you that you need to reach for the stars, go larger than life, uncover the fire inside you.

You strive for bigger 'whys', reasons that are more aspirational, more impressive. You now want to: become a millionaire; make the world a better place; achieve that elusive absolute freedom from a job you hate.

And you try again, only to fail again when your motivation evaporates—yet again.

"There must be something wrong with me," you think.

The truth is, there is nothing wrong with you. The truth is, you have been misled.

Why 'motivate yourself' advice often fails

The mainstream approach to goal setting and motivation assumes you know what lights your fire.

Motivational experts make you believe success is simply the matter of making a choice, and then setting your mind to it.

And while this may work for some people, it doesn't for everyone. This is because sometimes, those consciously chosen goals fail to be real motivators.

Simply speaking: it's not always a case of 'mind over matter'.

I had a client once, let's call her Jane. Ever since she was a child, Jane wanted to write novels.

She tried for many years to write her first novel, but somehow her efforts would fizzle out after a few weeks. At some point, she realised she had a problem with motivation.

She worked with a writing coach. She tried accountability groups, a contract with herself, all sorts. She signed up for NaNoWriMo (a world-wide event, where participants aim to complete a fifty-thousand-word novel in November) a few times. She always started with a great deal of enthusiasm and a solemn decision to complete her novel. Yet, she never finished the challenge. Her desk drawers and her computer drives were full of unfinished first drafts and outlines.

'I so, so want to write good stories,' she told me, 'but I can't'.

'Why do you want to write?' I asked her.

'Because I want to bring a little joy into people's lives', she said. 'I want to help to make the world a better place.'

That is a lovely reason to write. It's a laudable cause, isn't it?

Except for it wasn't true. The more we dug into Jane's motivations, the clearer it became that the real reason she wanted to write was to create plots, characters and rich intrigues, and see them unfold and resolve neatly.

What she wanted most was to write stories, and create worlds she could shape the way she wanted. She was driven to resolve problems she couldn't resolve in real life, and bring unfinished threads to a conclusion.

Now, this is a completely different story.

She told me she sort-of knew about her true desires but didn't want to be 'so selfish' in her pursuits. She had always thought that having a 'noble goal' and doing things for other people, would give her much more inspiration and motivation.

Except that, in her case, those 'adopted' reasons just hid what she really cared about. As a result, she wasted several years of her life trying to do something she craved, but for a reason she didn't really care about.

Oh, rats!

Your true heart's desire may not be what you think it is

Jane found her 'why' difficult to accept, because she felt it was selfish, and embarrassing.

And this is why traditional motivational approaches don't work for everyone.

Some people end up falling short of their goals, no matter how much they try.

Why?

Because like Jane, these people chose the right goals, for the wrong reasons.

Three motivational approaches that can kill your goals

Jane finally accepted her real motivation and since that time, she has been happily writing, completing and even publishing her stories. But if you're struggling like Jane used to, I have something that may be able to help you break through those invisible barriers.

Here are **the real reasons no one ever tells you about why your motivation is never enough.**

1.You're chasing your goals for other people's reasons and passions, not your own

You may be pursuing your own goals or dreams, but just like Jane, your reason doesn't come from your heart.

It may be because you're still being a 'good girl or boy' and fulfilling your parents' dreams.

You may have been told that pursuing a dream for yourself is morally wrong, or you're doing what's expected of you by your family, your community or societal/cultural norms. Or you may have even become so inspired by someone else's story, you decided you wanted to be like them—you fell into hero worship. You wanted so much to be fuelled by their fire, you have been telling yourself you care about it.

And even though you care about the book you're writing, having a healthier, lighter body, or setting up that business, the fuel you put behind your goal will not last long enough, because it is not your fuel.

Once you realise this, you may run into further difficulties.

2.You're scared or ashamed to embrace—or even discover—your real motivation

For whatever reasons, you are not allowing your real 'whys'–your deepest passions–to surface and drive your life.

Maybe you're afraid of them?

Maybe someone in your life doesn't accept them?

Or maybe you believe your motivational drivers aren't worthy, big, or good enough because everyone around talks about the importance of having an amazing mission. So, you, too, try to save the world, set yourself free, or become 'the best in town', even though this is not what you really want to achieve.

So, you have decided to believe you are driven by something else, something more ambitious, more inspirational.

But the sad truth is, if the motives you choose don't align with what matters to you on a deep, emotional level, you'll have to work much harder to achieve your goals (1). What's worse, there is a price for it, too—working towards the wrong goal can ruin your satisfaction with life (2). This is because it takes a tremendous amount of effort to make yourself believe those erroneous drivers.

There's one final, common mistake people make.

3.You're fooling yourself to be like other people

You want to be like your heroes, and you want it so badly, you adopt their motivational drivers, thinking this will get you to your dreams faster. You think you want to be like that amazing entrepreneur you heard on the podcast last week, or your super-fit friend, or your father, a dedicated doctor.

In an attempt to fit in, be accepted, or succeed like other people, you fooled yourself into believing you care about the stuff that, in fact, means very little to you.

But, sadly, it's the same problem. No matter how beautiful and aspirational those motivations are, no matter how powerful those reasons are, if they don't really light your fire, you are fooling yourself.

You just don't give a damn, no matter how much you tell yourself you do, and you are heading for failure.

It all comes down to one huge, glaring issue:

Pursuing the right goals for half-hearted, inauthentic reasons can jeopardise your success.

You may not be aware that what you think motivates you doesn't truly matter to you. You may know these are not your 'whys', but you're unable to change it, because the time is wrong, you care about the person the goal is important to, or you don't have enough courage to change it.

Or, you may know your motivators are all BS, but you're too scared to be true to yourself.

Admitting what really motivates you (even if only to yourself), is too difficult. It makes you feel overwhelmed, petrified, embarrassed, or even guilty.

But pursuing your goals for the wrong reason is depriving you of the success and happiness you deserve. It is not only failing to take you closer to your dreams, but it is also wasting your time and sucking energy out of you.

I've been there too.

Real reasons are tricky things.

For over 30 years, I tried hard to exercise regularly.

I wanted to do it to lose weight, to be healthier and fit, to look better. Sometimes it worked and sometimes it didn't. Mostly, it didn't.

A few years ago, (around the time I started working on my alternative career-changing plan), I hit a point where I was exhausted, extremely stressed, and struggled to focus on my job or even my other day-to-day activities. I desperately needed a break, but I also felt that if I stopped, I'd fall to pieces, and I'd find it impossible to pull myself together.

I needed an alternative plan. And I came up with one that featured regular exercise.

Yes, I had my own survival as my motivation for regular exercise. It doesn't get any more powerful than that, you might think. And you'd be right.

Survival is usually the turning point of a story like mine. The main character, faced with his/her own mortality, starts finally working toward his/her goal, fuelled by the powerful motivation of transforming his/her life.

But, this is not a typical inspirational story. Sorry! As I mentioned before, even my own survival was not enough to make me exercise regularly.

Was I stupid or crazy or what?

No.

That's because it is not as obvious and straightforward as all those aspirational-motivation stories make us think.

For many of us, the most powerful motivational driver is not always the one that appears to be the most powerful. And this was what happened in my case.

Faced with the risk of total physical, mental and emotional collapse, I 'came out' to myself. I finally admitted, that what I'd been telling myself I was 'passionate about' for all those years did not, in fact, make me feel fulfilled and happy.

Because what actually lights my fire, what really makes me tick, and what makes me get lost in a task and keep going despite the worst obstacle is something else.

I'm not particularly proud of it, but hey—this is the way I am.

Here I am, Joanna, an achievement junkie, with a penchant for **Mastery.**

The moment I set up my exercise routine to fuel it by what really motivates me, it started running like a well-oiled machine.

It's been nearly three years, and I still run three times a week, rain, shine or frost, even though I still hate running.

Admitting to myself that I'm motivated by my love of mastery more than anything else in life took me a long time and cost me an emotional burnout or two. And this may happen to you, too.

As I and others have said, pursuing goals driven by 'the wrong motivators' increases stress, affects your emotional and physical well-being, and sets you up for failure (3).

How to tap into powerful, lasting motivation

Opening your mind to explore what really motivates you, and embracing your real passion, can make a huge difference to your ability to achieve your goals. It may be difficult to accept, but it is the first, most important step to finally ditching the vicious cycle of goal setting failure. It will propel you on your way to success (4).

And you can finally lose weight and become fitter—like I did—get a better job, improve your relationships, or finish writing that book.

By discovering and admitting what truly motivates you, you can power your goals with long-lasting, powerful force that can help you move mountains, change habits you've been fighting for years.

Experience success.

Live in harmony with yourself.

Be happy again.

Plug into a potent source of power and move mountains

Being brutally honest with yourself about your motivation can save you many weeks, months or even years of frustration and failure to achieve your goals.

Recognising why you have chosen to pursue your goals for those specific reasons, even though they don't resonate with you is an important step. But that's just the beginning.

If you really want to succeed, acknowledge that the drivers and values that light your fire differ from the ones adopted from your parents, friends, or popular culture. Embrace those motivators and power your goals with them. Doing this can create a powerful shift in your life.

And the best thing is, nobody needs to know what your true passion is! You don't have to tell anyone. You don't have to change your plans, just change the source of power to fuel the pursuit of your goals.

How can you accomplish this switch? Often, it's just a matter of wording

For example, you want to exercise daily to build your mastery in running longer distances (your real motivation) and not just to be able to play with your kids (your 'adopted' driver). Alternatively, you might want to improve your productivity to have more time to explore other passions, instead of trying to free yourself from the 9-to-5 shackles.

Of course, you can still use your improved fitness to play more with your kids. You can also harness the extra time you gained through improved productivity to build your part-time business. But the reason why you're working towards your goals, your motivation is now aligned with things that *really* light your fire.

This approach has worked both for me and the many clients I've helped rediscover and 'come out', with regards to their real motivation in life.

Change your life by embracing your true motivation

Now you are aware how adopting the wrong motivation can prevent you from achieving your goals, don't be afraid to look beyond what you've accepted as 'right'.

Look into your heart. Thinking about why you want to achieve your goal is not enough, you have to feel that desire in every fibre of your being. You have to believe your reasons with your whole heart.

This is where the real, lasting motivation lies.

Tap into what truly lights your fire, and your dreams will be fuelled by a powerful force, a force that will drive you to your goals almost effortlessly, faster than you ever believed possible. And, at last—deep in your heart—you will feel at peace with yourself, happy and fulfilled.

PART IV

POPULAR MOTIVATIONAL STRATEGIES AND HOW TO USE THEM

13

HABITS AND SYSTEM BUILDING

This chapter was originally written for my Hack Your Habits book. I have adapted it to help you understand how you can use systems and habit to keep your motivation going.

I n this section of the book, I'll look at some common motivational strategies, I'll discuss when they may be helpful, and when you should avoid them.

I'll start by presenting you my favourite 'motivational strategy', habit system building. I put 'motivational strategy' in the quotation marks, because this is not really a motivational strategy, but rather, another way of using your well-defined and correctly-targeted motivation.

Usually, when you first set a goal, you are excited and enthusiastic about it, and you feel you can move mountains. This energy can be quite powerful, however using it to work on your goal is not the right strategy.

The secret power of systems on autopilot

Human memory is prone to error, distortions and, in general, can fail to supply the right information at the right time. This is why, if you want something to work every time, you shouldn't rely on your memory. The best way to ensure that the right thing happens at the right time, is to build it into an autopilot system.

Without doubt, autopilot systems are better at ensuring the right things happen at the right time and in the right way.

These systems can have various forms, processes, algorithms, standard operating procedures, etc. They are created to achieve not only efficiency, but also high quality of output, uniformity of performance, and to make sure the task is performed every single time it needs to be done.

Decision-support systems are associated with improvements in clinical practice (1) and clinician's performance (2). The importance of having good, reliable systems in place that eliminate or minimise human error, or its effect on safety, has been well documented in many industries where safety is paramount, such as medicine and aviation (3).

Systems can guide your decision-making processes, or simply force you to take a predetermined option. For example, in machines used in anaesthesia, during surgical procedures (patient monitoring etc.), a pin safety system prevents the attachment of the wrong cylinder to the wrong outlet and delivery of the wrong gas. In this case, the parts simply won't fit if you try to plug the wrong gas to the wrong point (4). 'Dead man switches' play a similar role in many machines and vehicles (5). Using these systems, if the operator is no longer in control of the machine, the machine stops working.

Systems are smarter than human nature

Systems take into consideration the most common ways in which humans make mistakes and either eliminate, or minimise the likelihood of mistakes happening. To put it bluntly, systems are designed to outsmart human weak points.

Do you have problems with making choices and it slows you down? Put a system in place that takes that burden out of your hands and speeds up your progress towards your goal. I run three times a week: Tuesdays, Thursdays and Saturdays. So, if it's Saturday, I'm going for a run—even if it's raining and cold. I don't have to check if I'm motivated, or worry about my willpower levels. This is just what I do on Saturday morning—I run.

I've successfully built systems to get up early, eat better, take notes from books I read, etc. I've also helped other people create systems for improving their focus, eliminating distractions and fighting procrastination, and creating a regular writing routine, etc.

This is why I believe creating systems that make you take a predetermined action, can accelerate your journey towards your self-improvement goals, and towards creating better habits in particular.

The systems I help my clients and students create, take into consideration their quirks, preferences, strengths and weaknesses (particularly weaknesses!), as well as the constraints and limitations of their physical, emotional, and social environments. I suggest ways to design these systems to guide, nudge, and even force my clients, (with their consent, of course!), to take actions leading towards their goals.

Below is a quick summary of my approach to building systems/habits to work towards long-term goals. For more information, check my book *Hack Your Habits*.

Hack Your Motivation the *Hack Your Habits* Way

1. Make sure your goals are realistic and achievable

I've covered this principle in depth before (Chapter 7), so I'll only provide a very brief refresher here:

- Make sure your goals are still realistic and achievable, because if they are not, you're either setting yourself up to fail, or you will end up constantly dreaming of a better life/better you, or both
- Explore your current context and your personality to make sure your goal fits in with both
- Don't ignore your constraints and limitations, pay attention to other goals—particularly those competing for your time and energy
- Look at what you can realistically achieve here and now, not next week, or once you've lost that weight or children have left the nest

2. Make your plan on a neutral or a bad day

I know, it sounds really mean, but many people told me this was one of the best pieces of advice they've received when it came to setting goals. Plan your goal-achievement strategy on a neutral (normal) or even a bad day. When you're busy, tired, after a bad night's sleep, you're more likely to be realistic about your chosen strategies. If you make a plan you can execute on a normal day, then you have a much greater chance of following through and achieving your goal.

3. Assume there will be temptations and plan for them

As I explained before, one of the main dangers of planning how to achieve your goals while you are super motivated, is that you become unrealistic and assume you will always feel as invincible. As a result, you also tend to underestimate potential temptations not to follow through with your plan, assuming you'll be able to deal with them.

'It's really easy to agree to a diet if you're not hungry,' (6)

This quote from Baumeister is one of my favourite and rightly so. It reflects what tends to happen in a situation called **'cold-hot empathy gap'**. When in a cold, rational state of mind, we tend to undermine the strengths of 'hot', visceral drivers, such as hunger, sexual desire, and tiredness. That's why we tend to think we'll be able to overcome them with the sheer strength of our willpower.

The reason why I don't waste my day away web surfing even though my workspace appears to be allowing that, is not because I'm a self-restraint superhero. Of course, I have a motivation to write, but I also have crappy willpower. On top of that, as I explained earlier, I have to feed my 'instant gratification monkey' every so often. As a result, I tend to take frequent breaks. But my productivity system knows what I tend to do and what I will not do and is set up in a way that limits the *doing* and promotes the *not-doing*. For instance, I'm free to browse the Internet when I'm working, but I'm logged out of all but three sites. I can quickly check these three sites (my email, a social media account and one of my sales reports), but if I wanted to check anything else, I'd have to dig up the login details and log in. More often than not, this is just too much effort for me and I don't do it.

Similarly, I don't spend hours going through my emails, because I have a 2-minute rule in place and it relies on my laziness. Once I open an email, I triage it into: Delete, Defer, or Reply Immediately. I only reply immediately to the messages that take less than 2 minutes to write. Anything longer is deferred to the email answering slots in my timetable.

Unless you have iron-clad willpower, well-tested over the years, I suggest you assume there will be temptations and prepare for them, as if they occur daily. Plan for them, eliminate as many as you can, and limit the impact of those you can't eliminate.

4. Address resistance upfront

Resistance is another issue you need to be aware of and stay ahead of. And, like temptations, pretending this will not be an issue, is foolish. Unless you never have any problems with resistance (which typically manifests as procrastination), you'd better prepare for it.

The specific resistance-boosting approach you use will depend on the reason for your resistance. Why are you dragging your feet? Are you overwhelmed by the size of the task, or is it the fear of failure or success? Or maybe you are driven by perfectionism (usually a derivative from one of the above)?

You need to identify the underlying reasons for your resistance/procrastination, and put an appropriate strategy to deal with it upfront.

5. Focus on habits

The biggest challenge with attaining long-term goals, is not the fact they take long to achieve. It's not even the delayed gratification. In my experience, it's the fact that many of those goals require us to change our behaviour, often, a well-engrained, habitual behaviour. Eating certain foods, leaving things to the last minute, or spending money on things we don't need, all fall into this category. Many people fail at achieving their goals, because they don't see those changes as necessary and focus on the surface issues.

Behavioural change is challenging. It takes a long time to happen and, did I say it's hard? Yes, and the longer you have been ingraining the behaviour, the harder it will be to change it.

That's why many long-term goal plans would fare better, if the planner considered them from the point of view of habits that need to be changed.

So, you want to lose weight? Start with an exercise routine and good eating habits.

You want to save up for a deposit on a house? Look at your spending patterns, and get into a habit of saving regularly.

Examine your current habits and consider what you need to change to improve them. For more information on habit building and changing, check my book *Hack Your Habits*.

What is the habit building approach best used for?

Building habit systems that help you achieve your goals works very well for any goals that require behavioural change or long-term commitment and several weeks, months, years of repeating the same/similar behaviour. If you want to lose weight through healthy eating, you can create a system that forces you to eat more healthily. If you want to become fit and healthy by exercising, an exercise routine system can help you succeed. The same goes for productivity goals that can take you to your next career move, or a reading routine to support your educational goals.

When it may not be a good idea to use this approach

Conversely, don't use the habit-building approach to work on goals that require one-off actions or actions that can be repeated only once in a while (e.g. a few times per year). Sometimes, heroic actions once in a while are less time- and energy-consuming than creating a system that you won't be using too often.

Be careful however. If you are considering something that requires a long-term commitment, but it appears to consist of once-in-a-while actions—such as preparing and filling your yearly tax return—explore if there are some other behaviours that could make those big once-off events easier. For example, to do a yearly tax return (a stressful event for many of us), it may be not worth it, however you may make it much easier if you create a habit of filing all your receipts and payslips accurately throughout the year.

Hopefully, I've convinced you to try a habit building approach when working on behaviour-changing long-term goals. In the next chapter, I'll talk about willpower—when and why it may work, and when to avoid using it as your 'motivational strategy'.

Action point:

Part 4 of this book contains a number of popular motivational strategies. Please read chapters 13 - 18 and consider which of the presented strategies may be helpful in achieving your goals, and which are better avoided. Record your responses in Section III of the Workbook.

Following this Chapter, answer the corresponding questions on page 9 of the Workbook:

- What motivational strategies are likely to help me achieve my goal?

- What strategies should I avoid?

- What strategies can I try?

- Have I used habit/system building strategies successfully in the past?

- Can I successfully use habit/system-building strategies while pursuing this goal?

- What can I do to make habit-/system-building strategies more effective?

14

WILLPOWER AND SELF-CONTROL

Willpower and self-control (these two concepts are very similar and are often used interchangeably) are commonly recommended as motivation substitutes. As more and more people become aware that relying on motivation to achieve long-term goals is not a sustainable strategy, they try to use willpower instead.

This can be a very good strategy, because while motivation is unreliable, you can always force yourself to perform an action with the sheer power of your self-control.

That is, if you can.

Unfortunately, willpower and the ability to force yourself to do things that don't bring immediate rewards, appear unpleasant, too difficult, or too costly, is a dying art.

Being able to control your attention, emotions, and desires, is a vital ingredient of any recipe for success. This is true in both your personal and professional lives. Without self-control, you will be constantly at the mercy of your impulses. You may end up eating donuts, watching Netflix for hours on end, playing Candy Crush all day, and thereby, jeopardise your health, relationships, financial security, and professional reputation, as well as kill your self-improvement goals.

I agree with the principle that willpower is more reliable than motivation, because even when you don't feel motivated, you can always force yourself to carry on. And there is little doubt that many people are able to push themselves forward with the sheer strength of their willpower, 'muscling their way through the pain'.

So, it might sound as though willpower is a great strategy for helping yourself achieve your goals.

And it is.

Except for when it isn't.

Unfortunately, as Kelly McGonigal, the world-renowned health psychologist writes (1)—many traditional approaches to using willpower are ineffective, and may even backfire leading to self-sabotage instead of help.

Willpower has its pitfalls.

Willpower outages happen

The most common problem is **willpower (or ego) depletion.**

Although, a recent study challenges this theory (2), a body of research (3) argues that we have a limited supply of willpower in our 'willpower containers'. And just like with water or fuel tanks, every time you use some of that willpower from your tank, there is less left for later. The amount of willpower will not increase, until you are able to replenish it.

That's why it's so hard to resist that chocolate bar in the vending machine after a particularly difficult meeting, or a lengthy shopping trip. It takes self-discipline and willpower to do so.

Although new studies are emerging, challenging this long-held belief about willpower depletion, personally, I have experienced moments when my willpower is down and I'm aware of typical situations that are likely to cause it. That's why I believe that understanding how to use willpower is important to an individual's ability to work toward long-term goals.

For example, a common process that requires a great deal of willpower is decision making. Why? Because decision-making is about careful consideration of various aspects of the choices you have. You need to weigh up pros and cons of your options. Should you choose a cheaper, but less reliable brand of washing machine, or more expensive and sturdier? Should you pay the total and use the credit card, or should you use financing? A 12-month finance, or a 24-one? And so on.

If you want to avoid making a bad decision, you need to put quite a lot of thinking into the process. And the more options you have to go through, the more trade-offs you need to balance, the harder your decision-making muscles work, and the more willpower you drain from your tank.

Let's now look at the situations when using willpower can work well, and when willpower is unlikely to help you achieve your goals.

What are willpower-based approaches best for?

First of all, if you generally have good willpower/self-control, then obviously, you're more likely to succeed using this strategy than someone like me, who has almost none . It is worth mentioning that according to some studies, willpower can be strengthened if you practice self-control regularly, by doing even simple exercises (4, 5).

Interestingly, some people are able to push themselves harder, if they know the results of the task they are working on will benefit others, or themselves. (6)

This would suggest people with purpose-driven goals (or those who clearly understand what they are getting from the task they are working on), may be able to use willpower-based strategies with success.

Another study suggests that people who believe their willpower is unlimited generally do better on tasks that require controlling themselves and straining decision-making 'muscles' (7).

So, if you have the willpower mind-set, or are able to adopt this approach, you may want to try this strategy.

When it may not be a good idea to use this approach

Over the centuries, strategies relying on self-discipline and willpower worked. But in modern times, we face more temptations than ever before (8), with fast food, fast cash, abundance of products and services available at a click of a mouse/button, our self-discipline is constantly 'under fire'. To make things worse, many of us are not equipped to deal with self-control issues. With more disposable income and credit cards widely available, lack of money is often not perceived as a barrier. The 'you deserve it and you deserve it now' mantra is also often used as a way to push us to buy, or do things that may not necessary be good for us, only because 'we deserve it'.

Traditionally, self-control used to be taught at home, at school, or in the church/religious environment. This is not happening as much as it used to, particularly in western societies. As a result, many people are left feeling inadequately equipped to deal with the temptations of the modern, consumer-centric world.

If you're someone who struggles with self-control, I'd recommend you find other strategies for keeping you on track towards your goals.

As already discussed, I usually build habit systems to eliminate or limit temptations and cut through resistance. This is also what I recommend to my students and clients with willpower issues.

Alternatively, you might like to consider training your willpower. There are a number of resources out there to help you develop willpower. I have included a couple of chapters on willpower in my *Hack Your Habits* book, as well as some more further reading resources.

Action point:

This chapter corresponds to Section III of the Workbook (page 9-10).

Answer the following questions and record your responses in the Workbook:

- Have I used willpower strategies successfully in the past?

- Can I use willpower/self-control approach while pursuing this goal?

- What can I do to make willpower/self-control strategies more effective?

15

INSPIRATIONAL STORIES, SPEECHES, AND QUOTES

This chapter focuses on probably the most popular strategy for boosting your motivation—**reading and listening to inspirational stories, speeches, quotes** etc.

There is an abundance of books, articles, films, etc. with stories of people overcoming unbelievable obstacles and working hard to achieve their goals. The same goes for inspirational quotes and images. Who hasn't got them on the wall (a physical, or a social media one), their computer desktop, or somewhere else in the office/house? Even I used to have a collection of quotes up in my bedroom. If you remember, that's the one that ended up in the bin.

We love those stories. We love those quotes and images. Why? The simple answer is because they inspire us to rise above our current situation. They give us hope that we too, will succeed. They push us to work on our own weaknesses and leave our comfort zones behind.

How do these stories boost our motivation?

I've conducted some research and to be honest, got lost myself. It appears that their motivation-boosting ability has something to do with the power that stories have over us, through evoking emotions. It probably goes back to those campfire tales of scary monsters and heroic pursuits to fend them off our ancestors told to pass the long, dark nights.

Emotions are the engines that push us to act. Whether it's a fight or flight response or warm feelings from watching a cat video, these emotional experiences give us energy boosts that we want to channel somewhere. Very often, this energy is channelled into action.

This is all great, but sadly, these emotional states don't last too long. I'm sure there are people who, inspired by the examples of others, have gone onto transform their lives, and that's fantastic. Unfortunately, I have also met many, many people, who, initially inspired, embarked on a journey toward great goals, only to find themselves deprived of motivation and slipping back to square one again.

I have been there too many times in my younger life. I'm guilty of falling for weight-loss 'miraculous strategies' shared by others, or 'this is how I discovered my real passion' stories. At some point, after several failures, I realised these stories, however good they made me feel, did not lead to sustainable action.

In a nutshell: **inspirational stories have the power to evoke strong emotions in us. Emotions push us to action,** and that's why we find **inspirational stories motivating.**

However, emotions, by nature, are short-lived. If you don't back your efforts with sustainable actions, you will quickly end up on a 'motivational low', and you'll need another 'booster' to keep going. This is why so many people who use inspirational stories to 'get motivated', struggle to achieve long-term goals, and become victims of never ending 'stop-restart' cycles.

It also appears that the better we are at identifying inspiration-driven emotions that affect us, the less they seem to fuel our intrinsic motivation (1). As a result, those of us who are emotionally intelligent, may be less likely to benefit from motivational properties of inspirational stories.

What are inspirational approaches best used for?

I'd like to leave this decision up to you. If reading/listening to inspirational stories, gives you a motivational boost and you enjoy it, be mindful that its effect is not likely to last long. So, use this positive energy to build a system that will have you reach your goals (see Chapter 13 for more info), and/or find another strategy to keep your motivation going.

When it may not be a good idea to use this approach

Conversely, if these don't work for you, stop wasting your time and energy on looking for yet another story to inspire you. Also, the better you are at understanding and managing your emotions, the less likely you are to benefit from this approach.

Action point:

This chapter corresponds to Section III of the Workbook (pages 10-11).

Answer the following questions and record your responses in the Workbook:

- Have I used inspirational speeches, stories and quotes as a motivational strategy successfully in the past?

- Can I use them effectively while working on this goal?

- What can I do to make this strategy more effective?

- What speeches/stories/quotes am I going to use?

16

EXTRINSIC REWARDS

I have spent a lot of time in this book telling you that if you really want a lasting motivation, you need to reach inside yourself. You need to find and plug yourself into your real intrinsic motivational driver(s).

But this is not to say that extrinsic motivators are bad and you should avoid using them.

Not at all.

In fact, I'm of the view that **extrinsic motivation can be used effectively in goal achievement**, too. However, you need to be quite careful about it.

I have covered this to some extent in Chapter 8, but I'd like to spend a few moments to remind you of the key information about extrinsic motivation.

Extrinsic motivation and extrinsic rewards are those drivers that are external to us, and not directly 'plugged' into our brain reward system. It means they don't act directly on the circuits in our brains, but we learn to associate them with the sensation of pleasure, or avoidance of something undesirable. So, because they act indirectly and require some additional effort to make them work, there are some issues with their effectiveness, particularly for longer-term goal attainment.

Below are **four rules that can help you make the most of extrinsic rewards.**

1. Use rewards that are attractive to you

It may sound obvious, but I am often asked questions about it from my readers. 'What's the best extrinsic reward to use?', or even 'I don't want to reward myself with chocolate, even though I love it, because I know chocolate is not good for me. So, I've been trying to use nice baths and aromatherapy sessions instead, but it's not really effective.'

I'm sorry to burst all the 'bath' bubbles 😊, but if the reward you choose for yourself, no matter how 'good for you' and acclaimed by others, is just not appealing enough, it's not going to work. I'll leave the choice and tests to you, but here's what works for me.

If I have to hit a deadline, I'll buy a packet of my favourite sweets and a teapot of my favourite earl grey tea, rather than the 'healthier options', and settle down to the task.

Honestly, the point of your rewards is to make you feel rewarded. If you don't, this is not a good reward.

If you're not sure what may work for you, try various rewards and keep an eye on their effectiveness on you. It's good to have a range of little tactics 'up your sleeve', to avoid 'reward fatigue'. You can try positive or negative reinforcements to test which of those may work better for you. For example, I use mainly sweets/little pleasures (positive reinforcement), and only resort to loss-avoidance when I have a truly binding deadline, (e.g. when I'm doing something for someone, or in the case of a writing assignment, a contest entry etc.).

2. Use them when you need them

Given the limited lasting effect of extrinsic motivation, it's best to use it only when absolutely necessary, e.g. on bad days, or when you have to hit a deadline. Be careful to return to your main intrinsic driver as soon as you can. As I have often said, the effect of extrinsic rewards tends to wear off over time ('reward fatigue').

3. Change the rewards when you notice they are not effective enough

Unlike intrinsic drivers, extrinsic motivators have a limited life span. That's why I recommend using them sparingly. However, if, despite your smart approach to extrinsic motivators, you find yourself realising that money, praise, chocolate, or aromatherapy (to name but a few), are no longer as effective as they used to be, consider trying something else.

Test a variety of rewards. You can try rewards of the same type, e.g. if you've successfully used money before, you can try a money equivalent (e.g. vouchers, material prizes). Or, you can experiment with a different type of reward, such as non-monetary praise, for example getting 'upvotes' on your social media posts sharing your success.

4. Beware of the overlap with your intrinsic drivers

Sadly, combining the two types of motivation may sometimes work against you. Using extrinsic rewards to boost a desired behaviour that is driven internally, is potentially a dangerous situation.

Over-justification effect (also known as 'motivation crowding

theory') is the reason people, who enjoy doing stuff for the fun of it, stop enjoying the same thing once they get paid for it (2). If you think yourself lucky getting a job where you'll be pursuing your passion and get paid a lot of money and other perks for it, you may actually be in danger of losing that sense of enjoyment and fulfilment.

Be mindful how your motivation works, and keep an eye on your extrinsic rewards, so that they don't overpower your internally driven joy and undermine your efforts (3).

What are extrinsic rewards best for?

To reiterate what I've said above, extrinsic rewards are best used sparingly. Keep them for situations when you need that extra push to start, or to keep going, at an (unrewarding) task.

You're likely to need extrinsic rewards when you're working on something you have little interest in, when you're tired or otherwise not in top form, but you still have to work. Sometimes, a little pleasure can help you push through a difficult moment, or complete a project ahead of the deadline. But make sure you stop using the reward as soon as it's no longer necessary (or effective).

When it may not be a good idea to use extrinsic rewards

As you can probably imagine, using extrinsic rewards too often is likely to result in a reduction in effectiveness of those rewards, or even in a reversal of your intrinsic drivers. Also, because of the impact of over-justification effect, avoid using extrinsic motivators to push yourself to do what you normally enjoy doing.

Extrinsic rewards can work well, if used wisely. So be wise and enjoy them!

Action point:

This chapter corresponds to Section III of the Workbook (pages 11-12).

Answer the following questions and record your responses in the Workbook:

- Have I used extrinsic rewards as a motivational strategy successfully in the past?

- What type of extrinsic rewards have I responded to well in the past?

- Can I use them effectively while working on this goal?

- What other extrinsic rewards can I use if necessary?

17

VISUALISATION

Who doesn't like visualising their goals? This is particularly true if it involves achieving something extraordinary, like becoming a millionaire, building an app with Artificial Intelligence, or mastering five languages to the native level. Feels good, doesn't it?

It does, for me.

As a kid, and then a young adult, I used to spend a lot of time daydreaming like that. And then I read this was a popular motivation-boosting strategy called 'visualisation', and it had been proven very effective in goal achievement. So, I started doing more and more of it.

To be honest, it didn't end up well. Despite my best efforts, I am yet to win a Nobel Prize in literature, or become a world-famous scientist.

Visualisation is a popular motivational strategy. Almost every book on motivation and goal-setting I've read included visualisation as one of the most important strategies. Why? Because, as many studies suggest (1, 2), **visualisation is an effective goal-achievement strategy, particularly when it comes to sports activities.**

Apparently, when you visualise yourself landing that ball in the basket, or crossing the finish line, is makes your brain 'practise' the action. By simply imagining yourself as reaching the goal, your brain creates neural pathways and your body is primed to act. So, you get to practise the action leading to your desired outcome before you actually do it. This increases your confidence and comfort level.

Additionally, imagining yourself overcoming obstacles on your way to your goal may be quite effective in boosting your self-efficacy not only in terms of your mind-set, but also practically. Simply thinking through your strategies for reaching your goal can help you discover potential difficulties. Being more aware of risks, and moreover, addressing potential problems or minimising their impact on your success, actually increases your chances of success.

Sadly, I have never achieved any of the goals I have visualised so many times in the past. So, I started to suspect that visualisation may not work for everyone or for every goal. If you've noticed regardless of how much you imagine yourself achieving your ideal weight, winning that prize, or wowing your boss with your presentation, and your goal remains as distant as before, you're not alone.

Why is this so? Why does this happen?

While there may be a number of factors at play in each case, recent evidence suggests that sometimes, visualisation may not only be ineffective, but it may actually work against goal acquisition (3).

Apparently, sometimes, or for some people, visualising success drains the energy out of the motivation for that very goal. These people feel they have already achieved their goal, so they enjoy that feeling of glory and triumph and ... relax. In fact, they relax so much, they never achieve their goal. The research suggests that these individuals don't bother striving for their goals because, in their minds, they've already attained them!

Weird, eh?

More dangerously, a study (3) discovered that the more pressing the need to succeed, the bigger the effects of 'energy drain'. In one of the investigated experiments, a thirsty individual who visualised a glass of water, was able to trick his brain into thinking he had actually drunk the water.

As you can imagine, the consequences of such behaviour could be devastating.

What is visualisation best used for?

The available evidence suggests visualisation helps improve sports performance in those who are already good at the skills required. Hence, visualisation may work when you already have the skills, but you need a mental booster to your self-esteem or confidence level. Visualisation may be able to provide that boost and help you achieve your goals a little faster.

When it may not be a good idea to use this approach

If you realise your visualisation turns into daydreaming sessions, stop. This is what happened in my case. I loved thinking up various scenarios in which I achieved my goals, but, as I mentioned before, it did not help me much. In fact, visualisation was more of a hindrance. I wasted too much time and energy doing so. The moment I stopped day-dreaming and started just getting on with my plans, my pace towards success accelerated.

As always, I encourage you to test and discover what works best for you.

Action point:

This chapter corresponds to Section III of the Workbook (page 12).

Answer the following questions and record your responses in the Workbook:

- Have I used visualisation as a motivational strategy successfully in the past?

- Can I use it effectively while working on this goal?

- What specific visualisations can I use?

18

ACCOUNTABILITY AND OTHER SOCIAL STRATEGIES

I f you have ever used an accountability buddy, or joined a support group to achieve a goal, you will be familiar with the motivational approaches I describe in this chapter. **Social strategies**, as I call them, **are commonly used to boost motivation**, particularly when it comes to long-term goals and habit-building.

For many people, it's easier to achieve a long-term goal or implement a major behavioural change, if they have the support of others. Often, when you're trying to implement a lifestyle change, involving your family, friends or flatmates is important because of the support they can offer you. Another advantage of having key people on board is that they don't make it harder for you, by offering you the foods you're trying to avoid, or coming to chat to you at times when you're working.

Let's look at some popular social strategies.

1. Accountability-based strategies

These strategies rely on having someone keep you accountable explicitly or implicitly.

- **Accountability buddy/group/coach**

In this scenario, you ask a person or a group of people directly and explicitly to keep you accountable. Here, you are expected to check in with your accountability partner(s) and give them an update on your progress. This type of interaction is often reciprocal, as the other person expects you to do the same for them. This strategy may also involve the support of others in the group.

- **Implicit social contracts**

This approach is less direct, and many people find it less binding. Typically, this involves simply sharing your plans/goals with your friends, family, work colleagues, etc. These days, you can also do this on social media. There are no nominated people who check on your progress, and no expectation to report on success or failure. However, disclosing your plans to other people creates an expectation that you will progress towards your goal.

Many people have also used social media, blogs etc. to record their journey towards their goals and keep themselves accountable.

- **Commitment contracts/devices**

Commitment devices are strategies using accountability and social contracts, mixed with a number of other approaches. Often, there is no specific person to be accountable to, and most often the contract the user signs, is with themselves. The contract is mediated/delivered via a service, app or other means and has a reward/punishment system attached to it. This way, it is supposed to be more binding.

It usually works like this:

You place a bet, pledge a sum of money, or make a commitment to achieve a goal. If you don't achieve your goal, you lose money (and any other rewards attached to it), or are subject to 'a punishment'. The punishment can be losing the money you've bet, or having a compromising message broadcasted to your friends/social networks.

A number of services, such as StickK, Gym-Pact (Pact) or Fatbet, etc., operate based on mechanisms like that.

How does it work?

Generally accepted wisdom is that making resolutions public, even if it's only disclosing it to friends or closest family members, helps individuals keep those commitments.

- Social support

One of the key mechanisms here is the social support that the person embarking on the journey receives from their accountability partners. Social support is extremely important when it comes to working towards a behavioural change, or a long-term goal, whether it a simple acceptance of the new behaviour, or a source of a 'boost to motivation'. A social supporter is that special someone who turns up on a rainy day and says, 'Come on, put your rain jacket on and we'll go for that walk.' It's the friendly ear at the other end of the phone line, who listens to your struggles with your diet, etc.

Social support can be a powerful motivational tool.

- Obligation to deliver

Another important factor at play is the actual accountability of having someone expecting something of you. For some people, the obligation to deliver on their promise is about being true to their beliefs, their identity, and it becomes a matter of personal integrity.

This is another reason why accountability strategies may provide a well-needed motivational boost.

- Loss aversion

For some people, the obligation to follow through on their commitment is fuelled by the need to avoid a loss of some sort. Loss here can include, a loss of face, reputation, or cause an embarrassment, or even shame. Loss aversion is an interesting psychological phenomenon that makes us consider a $1 lost as more important than $1 earned/gained.

Overall, accountability strategies often engender personal stakes on top, or alongside, the material cost of not keeping the commitment.

Does it work?

There is a great deal of evidence to support the idea that these strategies work. Obviously, having support for your goals is important to success. Loss aversion strategies have also been proven to work in a number of areas (1). However there is also a significant amount of evidence to show that the effectiveness of accountability strategies and contracts can be limited (2).

As indicated above, recent studies (3, 4) suggest that people who publicly commit to achieving **identity goals** are less likely to actually achieve those goals, because just talking about their goal made them think they've achieved it. By 'identity goals', I mean goals that influence the sense of who they are, e.g. career-related goals, behaviours linked with parenting, etc.).

Loss aversion, is even more complex, in my opinion. If you look at it from the extrinsic-intrinsic motivation perspective, loss aversion is clearly extrinsic in nature, and therefore, at high risk of having limited effectiveness.

Interestingly, some studies have shown even when people achieve their goals using loss aversion driven strategies (e.g. weight loss), they reverted to their previous behaviour and lost all the success they achieved, (in this case, they put all that lost weight back on).

2. Social contagion and social conformity strategies

These strategies explore the fact that, in general, **humans,** as social animals, **have a need to fit in and conform to social rules** (5). These unwritten rules make us behave in a similar manner to the people around us. So, if you're not a rebel by nature, these are also interesting motivational strategies to consider.

I'm sure many of you have experienced this in your youth—doing things because your friends were doing them, or because it was 'fashionable'. And while drinking, smoking or using all sorts of harmful substances because it's 'cool', or 'everyone in my group does it' is not a wise behaviour, it's important to understand how it works.

Jim Rohn famously said *'You are the average of the five people you spend most time with,'* (6). Indeed, evidence suggests that some of our behaviour 'spreads' through our social networks (7, 8). This phenomenon is called '**social contagion**'. Simply put, you can 'catch' a certain habit or a way of doing something from your friends, relatives or workmates. Apparently, one of the best ways to get yourself to exercise and eat more healthily is to surround yourself with people who do the same (9).

Given the above, common sense advice to surround yourself with people, who have achieved or are working towards the same goals, seems to make sense. This is likely to be particularly evident, if you are working towards giving up a bad habit. If you have ever tried to give up smoking, stop gossiping or cut down on your drinking, you will know how difficult this is to execute if you socialise with people who smoke, gossip, or spend a lot of time in bars.

3. Social identity strategies

Another little variation on the above social strategies is to associate yourself with a group of people who hold similar self-beliefs.

The mechanism believed to be at work here, is **social contagion, or social conformity**, but boosted with the individual's **sense of identity**. Once a person accepts they belong to a specific group of people, acting in accordance with those beliefs becomes a matter of personal integrity. Most people strive to maintain self-beliefs and preserve their integrity, and hence are more likely to follow through with their new, desired behaviours.

For example, if you start associating yourself with people who eat healthily because they value healthy food and care about their bodies, you assume this social identity. This way, eating a junk food takeaway will be more than breaking your promise to yourself and your group, it will go against who you are.

This can be a powerful strategy when used appropriately.

What are these strategies best for?

I have been exploring the usefulness of accountability and other social-based strategies recently. Social contagion theory seems to be well supported by the evidence, particularly when it comes to healthy behaviours in young adults. This seems to confirm my observation that surrounding yourself with people, who you want to be like may work well in those situations.

Commitment devices have also been proven effective to some extent. However, as I mentioned above, I have some reservations regarding their effectiveness, since they seem to rely heavily on extrinsic motivators. I suppose, the jury is still out on the long-term effectiveness of these strategies.

As for the **popular accountability approaches, I also have reservations regarding their usefulness.**

I need to make a 'conflict of interest' disclosure here.

I don't use accountability strategies because they don't work for me, except for instances when I set it up as a competitive challenge. This is because I am mainly **Mastery** and **Autonomy** driven. People who I speak to about using accountability seem to follow a similar pattern. Those, who find it effective, seem to be **Purpose**- or **Mastery**-driven, and those who find it of little benefit or don't use it at all, tend to be mostly **Autonomy**-driven.

This makes sense to me, at least on the surface. For people motivated by relationships with others and who have a strong sense of belonging, social contracts are connected with the deeper fabric of their identity. This is why, potentially, they have more to gain from fulfilling those contracts, and much more to lose from failing to deliver.

I have also seen accountability strategies work well with competitive individuals, whether this is a straightforward competition with their accountability buddy, or with themselves, with overcoming obstacles, or with reaching certain milestones. As you can probably guess, these are more likely to be **Mastery**-driven people.

Please, bear in mind, these are my observations derived from personal reflection and a number of conversations with other people. I haven't found yet any research to back it up, so feel free to test it and let me know how it all went for you.

When it may not be a good idea to use this approach

As I said above, I suspect the effectiveness of these strategies is linked to the main motivational drivers you identify with. I have no scientific evidence to support my conclusions, but if you are not a **Purpose**-driven person, or not exploring your competitive streak, you may want to consider whether using social strategies might work for you.

As always, I encourage you to test to see whether any of these strategies work for you, even if you're a **Mastery**- or **Autonomy**-motivated individual. However, if you have tried any of these strategies before, and didn't find them helpful, I suggest you may want to give them a pass.

I'm not a fan of commitment devices either. I am in the 'keep it to yourself' camp. I don't respond well to punishment (strategies based on loss avoidance) either. From experience, I'm not the only person to feel this way. Plus, given the extrinsic nature of the loss avoidance approach, I suppose its effectiveness can be limited.

However, if these work for you, go ahead, use them to your best advantage.

As with every other strategy and tactic I have presented in this book, use it if it works for you, and avoid it if it doesn't.

Action point:

This chapter corresponds to Section III of the Workbook (page 12-13).

Answer the following and additional questions and record your responses in the Workbook:

- Have I used accountability/other social strategies as a motivational strategy successfully in the past?

- Can I use them effectively while working on this goal?

- What specific accountability or social strategies can help me achieve this goal?

- What other accountability/ social strategies can I use while working on this goal?

CONGRATULATIONS!

You've made it to the end of this book. I hope you've discovered your very own powerful, lasting motivation to help you achieve any goals faster and with less effort. All that's left to do is to go and put it into practice.

If you don't take action on the things you've learnt and reflected on, none of it will make any difference to your success - whether it's your education, your personal or professional life. So, don't procrastinate - put your plan into action and power it with your true motivation.

Let me know how you're doing

I'm always keen to hear from my readers, so please let me know how the strategies presented in this book have worked for you. Please share your struggles, frustrations, and successes.

You can email me at: joanna@shapeshiftersclub.com

REFERENCES

Introduction
1. Koch, R. (2004). *Living the 80/20 way*. London: Nicholas Brealey.
2. Wood, W. and Neal, D. (2007). A new look at habits and the habit-goal interface. *Psychological Review*, 114(4), pp.843-863.
3. Tugend, A. (2010, Oct 09). Pumping Out the Self Control In the Age of Temptation. *The New York Times*; Accessed at: http://www.nytimes.com/2010/10/09/your-money/09shortcuts.html?_r=0
4. Jast, J. (2016). *Hack Your Habits. An Unusual Guide to Escape Motivational Traps, Bypass Willpower Problems, and Accelerate Your Success*. Kindle Edition.

Chapter 1: Motivation - Theory, 'Truths', and Myths
1. Chmielewski, B.J., (1745-1746), *New Athens or the Academy full of all science, divided into subjects and classes, for the wise ones to record, for the idiots to learn, for the politicians to practice, for the melancholics to entertain*; Quote accessed on 10 Sept 2017 at:
https://en.wikipedia.org/wiki/Nowe_Ateny
2. The Open University, (2016). *Motivation and factors affecting motivation*. The Open University. Kindle Edition.

3. Petri, H.L. and Govern, J.M. (2004). *Motivation. Theory, Research and Applications.* Fifth Edition. Wadsworth, Belmont, USA

Chapter 2: What Seems to Work
1. Stajkovic, A.D. and Luthans, F. (1997). A Meta-Analysis of the Effects of Organizational Behavior Modification on Task Performance, 1975–95; *Academy of Management Review*, vol. 40 no 5; p 1122-1149; doi: 10.2307/256929 http://amj.aom.org/content/40/5/1122.short
2. Petri, H.L. and Govern, J.M. (2004). *Motivation. Theory, Research and Applications.* Fifth Edition. Wadsworth, Belmont, USA
3. Pink, D.H. (2009). *Drive: The Surprising Truth About What Motivates Us.* New York, NY Riverhead Books

Chapter 3: What You Need to Know
1. Navarro, J. et al., (2013). Fluctuations in Work Motivation: Tasks do not Matter! *Nonlinear Dynamics, Psychology, and Life Sciences.* 17. 3-22.
2. Fogg, B.J. (quoted by Ramit Sethi) accessed on 17 September 2017 at: https://www.iwillteachyoutoberich.com/blog/how-to-motivate-yourself
3. Judge, T. A. et al., (1994). An empirical investigation of the predictors of executive career success (*CAHRS Working Paper #94-08*). Ithaca, NY: Cornell University, School of Industrial and Labor Relations, Center for Advanced Human Resource Studies; accessed on 17 September 2017 at: http://digitalcommons.ilr.cornell.edu/cgi/viewcontent.cgi?article=1232&context=cahrswp
4. Sheldon, K.M. and Kasser, T. (1998). Pursuing Personal Goals: Skills Enable Progress, but Not all Progress is Beneficial. *Personality and Social Psychology Bulletin,* pp. 1319-1331, v. 24, No. 12 ; AID - 10.1177/0146167298241206 [doi]; accessed on 17 September 2017 at: http://journals.sagepub.com/doi/abs/10.1177/0146167298241206
5. DeAngeles, T. (2003). Why We Overestimate Our Competence. *APA Monitor,* Vol 23, No. 2, accessed on 17 Sept 2017, at: http://www.apa.org/monitor/feb03/overestimate.aspx
6. https://www.verywell.com/what-is-extrinsic-motivation-2795164
7. https://www.verywell.com/what-is-intrinsic-motivation-2795385

8. Pink, D.H. (2009). *Drive: The Surprising Truth About What Motivates Us*. New York, NY Riverhead Books

Chapter 5: What's Your Fuel?
1. Petri, H.L. and Govern, J.M. (2004). *Motivation. Theory, Research and Applications*. Fifth Edition. Wadsworth, Belmont, USA
2. Pink, D.H. (2009). *Drive: The Surprising Truth About What Motivates Us*. New York, NY Riverhead Books
3. Adapted from Friesen C. (2016). *Achieve. Find Out Who You Are, What You Really Want, And How To Make It Happen*; Kindle Edition

Chapter 7: Make Sure You Have the Right Amount of Fuel
1. https://en.wikipedia.org/wiki/Delayed_gratification
2. https://en.wikipedia.org/wiki/Hyperbolic_discounting
3. Kahneman, D and Knetsch, J.L., Thaler, R.H. (1991). *Anomalies: The Endowment Effect, Loss Aversion, and Status Quo Bias. Journal of Economic Perspectives*, v.5, n.1-Winter 1991, pp. 193-206 Accessed; 15 September 2017; at: https://www.princeton.edu/~kahneman/docs/Publications/Anomalies_DK_JLK_RHT_1991.pdf

Chapter 8: Reward Yourself with What Motivates You
1. https://en.wikipedia.org/wiki/Motivation_crowding_theory

Chapter 10: Seven (Surprising) Reasons Why People Lose Motivation so Quickly
1. Navarro, J. et al., (2013). Fluctuations in Work Motivation: Tasks do not Matter! *Nonlinear Dynamics, Psychology, and Life Sciences*. 17. 3-22.
3. F Baumeister, Roy & Vohs, Kathleen. (1994). Self-Regulation, Ego Depletion, and Motivation. *Social Perspectives. Psychological Compass*. Vol. 1.

Chapter 11: Key Challenges and How to Deal with Them
1. Mischel, W. Shoda, Y. And Rodriguez, M.L. (1989). Delay of Gratification in Children. *Science*. Vol. 244, No. 4907 (May 26, 1989), pp. 933-

938, accessed on 18 September 2017 at:
http://www.jstor.org/stable/1704494

2. Urban, T. (2016). Inside the Mind of a Master Procrastinator, *TEDTalks*; accessed on 28 August at:
https://www.ted.com/talks/tim_urban_inside_the_mind_of_a_master_procrastinator

3. Baumeister, R.F. and Tierney, J. (2012). *Willpower: Rediscovering the Greatest Human Strength*. Penguin Press

4. Jast, J. (2016). *Hack Your Habits. An Unusual Guide to Escape Motivational Traps, Bypass Willpower Problems, and Accelerate Your Success.* Kindle Edition.

Chapter 12: The Great Motivational Hoax - Why Setting Powerful Goals Can Get You Nowhere

1. McClelland, D. C., Koestner, R., & Weinberger, J. (1989). How do self-attributed and implicit motives differ? *Psychological Review*, 96(4), 690-702. http://dx.doi.org/10.1037/0033-295X.96.4.690

2. Brunstein, J. C., Schultheiss, O. C., & Grässman, R. (1998). Personal goals and emotional well-being: The moderating role of motive dispositions. *Journal of Personality and Social Psychology*, 75(2), 494-508. http://dx.doi.org/10.1037/0022-3514.75.2.494 accessed on 17 September 2017; at: http://psycnet.apa.org/record/1998-10511-016

3. Baumann, N., Kaschel, R., & Kuhl, J. (2005). Striving for Unwanted Goals: Stress-Dependent Discrepancies Between Explicit and Implicit Achievement Motives Reduce Subjective Well-Being and Increase Psychosomatic Symptoms. *Journal of Personality and Social Psychology*, 89(5), 781-799.http://dx.doi.org/10.1037/0022-3514.89.5.781; Accessed on 19 September 2017, at: http://psycnet.apa.org/record/2005-15658-010

4. Hofer, J. Et al. (2010). Is Self-Determined Functioning a Universal Prerequisite for Motive–Goal Congruence? Examining the Domain of Achievement in Three Cultures. *Journal of Personality*, vol. 78(2), Blackwell Publishing, 1467-6494; http://dx.doi.org/10.1111/j.1467-6494.2010.00632.x; Accessed on 19 September 2017, at: http://onlinelibrary.wiley.com/doi/10.1111/j.1467-6494.2010.00632.x/abstract

Chapter 13: Habits and System Building

1. Kawamoto, K. et al. (2005), Improving Clinical Practice Using Clinical Decision Support Systems: A Systematic Review of Trials to Identify Features Critical to Success. *British Medical Journal*, 330:765 doi: http://dx.doi.org/10.1136/bmj.38398.500764.8F; Accessed at: http://www.bmj.com/content/330/7494/765.short

2. Garg, A.X. et al. (2005), Effects of Computerized Clinical Decision Support Systems on Practitioner Performance and Patient Outcomes: A Systematic Review. *JAMA.* 293(10):1223-1238. doi:10.1001/jama.293.10.1223. Accessed at: http://jama.jamanetwork.com/article.aspx?articleid= 200503

3. Latorella, K.A. and Prabhu P.V. (2000), A Review of Human Error in Aviation Maintenance and Inspection. *International Journal of Industrial Ergonomics,* Vol.26 (2), pp.133–161; Accessed at: http://www.sciencedirect.com/science/article/pii/00 2073738990014X

4. Subrahmanyam, M. and Mohan, S. (2013). Safety Features in Anaesthesia Machine. *Indian Journal of Anaesthesia*, 57(5), 472–480. http://doi.org/10.4103/0019-5049.120143; Accessed at: http://www.ncbi.nlm.nih.gov/pmc/articles/PMC3821264/

5. Wikipedia. (2016). Dead man's switch. [online] Available at: https://en.wikipedia.org/wiki/Dead_man%27s_switch [Accessed 19 Sept. 2017].

6. R. Baumeister, R.F. and Tierney, J. (2012). *Willpower: Rediscovering the Greatest Human Strength*. Penguin Press

Chapter 14: Willpower and Self-Control

1. McGonigal, K. (2012). *The willpower instinct.* New York: Avery.

2. Carter, E., Kofler, L., Forster, D., & McCullough, M. (2015). A Series of Meta-Analytic Tests of the Depletion Effect: Self-Control Does Not Seem to Rely on a Limited Resource. *Journal of Experimental Psychology*: General DOI: 10.1037/xge0000083

3. Baumeister, R., Bratslavsky, E., Muraven, M. and Tice, D. (1998). Ego depletion: Is the active self a limited resource? *Journal of Personality and Social Psychology,* 74(5), pp.1252-1265. Accessed at: http://www.ncbi.nlm.nih.gov/pubmed/9599441

4. Oaten, M., & Cheng, K. (2006). Longitudinal gains in self-regulation from physical exercise. *British Journal of Health Psychology*, 11, 717-733. Accessed on 15 Aug 2017 at https://www.ncbi.nlm.nih.gov/pubmed/17032494

5. Muraven, M. et al. (1999). Longitudinal improvement of self-regulation through practice: building self-control strength through repeated exercise. *Journal of Social Psychology*, 139, 446-457.

6. Muraven, M., & Slessareva, E. (2003). Mechanism of self-control failure: Motivation and limited resources. *Personality and Social Psychology Bulletin*, 29, 894–906. https://www.ncbi.nlm.nih.gov/pubmed/15018677

7. Bernecker, K., Herrmann, M., Brandstätter, V., & Job, V. (2015). Implicit theories about willpower predict subjective well-being. *Journal of Personality;* DOI: 10.1111/jopy.12225 (http://onlinelibrary.wiley.com/doi/10.1111/jopy.12225/abstract)

8. Tugend, A. (2010, Oct 09). Pumping Out the Self Control In the Age of Temptation. *The New York Times;* Accessed at: http://www.nytimes.com/2010/10/09/your-money/09shortcuts.html?_r=0

Chapter 15: Inspirational Stories, Speeches, and Quotes

1. Vandercammen L, Hofmans J, Theuns P., (2014). Relating Specific Emotions to Intrinsic Motivation: On the Moderating Role of Positive and Negative Emotion Differentiation. *PLOS ONE* 9(12): e115396. https://doi.org/10.1371/journal.pone.0115396; Accessed on 15 Aug, 2017

Chapter 16: Extrinsic Rewards

2. Kohn, A. (1993). Why Incentive Plans Cannot Work. *Harvard Business Review*, September/October https://hbr.org/1993/09/why-incentive-plans-cannot-work

3. Tang, S.-H. and Hall, V. C. (1995), The overjustification effect: A meta-analysis. *Applied Cognitive Psychology*, 9: 365–404. doi:10.1002/acp.2350090502 http://onlinelibrary.wiley.com/doi/10.1002/acp.2350090502/full

4. Deci, E.L., Koestner, R and Ryan, R.M., (1999). A meta-analytic review of experiments examining the effects of extrinsic rewards on intrinsic motivation. *Psychological Bulletin*. Vol. 125(6):627-68

Chapter 17: Visualisation
1. David Shearer et al. (2009), The Effects of a Video-Aided Imagery Intervention upon Collective Efficacy in an International Paralympic Wheelchair Basketball Team. *Journal of Imagery Research in Sport and Physical Activity*, vol. 4 issue 1; DOI: 10.2202/1932-0191.1039; Accessed on 12 August 2017 at:
https://www.researchgate.net/publication/229009329
2. Parnabas V et al. (2015), The Influence of Mental Imagery Techniques on Sport Performance among Taekwondo Athletes. *European Academic Research*, Vol.2 (11); Accessed on 17 September 2017 at:
http://euacademic.org/UploadArticle/1396.pdf
3. Kappes, H B, Oettingen G. (2011), Positive fantasies about idealized futures sap energy. *Journal of Experimental Social Psychology*, vol 47, issue 4, https://doi.org/10.1016/j.jesp.2011.02.003) Accessed on 19 September 2017 at:
http://www.sciencedirect.com/science/article/pii/S002210311100031X

Chapter 18: Accountability and Other Social Strategies
1. Kahneman, D. & Tversky, A. (1984). "Choices, Values, and Frames" (PDF). *American Psychologist*. 39 (4): 341–350. doi:10.1037/0003-066x.39.4.341; accessed on 14 Sept. 2017 at: http://psycnet.apa.org/journals/amp/39/4/341/
2. John, L.K., Loewenstein, G., Troxel, A.B. et al. (2011). Financial Incentives for Extended Weight Loss: A Randomized, Controlled Trial. *Journal of General Internal Medicine*, vol. 26: 621. Accessed on 17 September on: https://doi.org/10.1007/s11606-010-1628-y
https://link.springer.com/article/10.1007/s11606-010-1628-y
3. Markman, A. (2009). If you want to succeed, don't tell anyone. *Psychology Today*. Accessed on 17 August 2017, at: https://www.psychologytoday.com/blog/ulterior-motives/200905/if-you-want-succeed-don-t-tell-anyone

4. Gollwitzer, P. M et al. (2009): When Intentions go Public. Does Social Reality Widen the Intention-Behaviour Gap? *Psychological Sciences*, vol. 20 (5)

5. Tomasello, M. (2014), The ultra-social animal. *European Journal of Social Psychology*, vol.44: 187–194. doi:10.1002/ejsp.2015; accessed on 15 August 2017, at: http://onlinelibrary.wiley.com/doi/10.1002/ejsp.2015/full

6. https://www.goodreads.com/quotes/1798-you-are-the-average-of-the-five-people-you-spend

7. Hruschka, D.J., et al. (2011). Shared Norms and Their Explanation for the Social Clustering of Obesity. *American Journal of Public Health*. December 2011. Accessed on 12 September 2017 at: http://ajph.apha-publications.org/doi/full/10.2105/AJPH.2010.300053

8. Christakis, N.A. and Fowler, J.H. (2012). Social contagion theory: examining dynamic social networks and human behavior. *Statistics in Medicine*; vol. 32 (4); pp: 1097-0258; accessed on 19 September at: http://dx.doi.org/10.1002/sim.5408

9. Barclay, K.J., Edling, C. And Rydgren J. (2013). Peer clustering of exercise and eating behaviours among young adults in Sweden: a cross-sectional study of egocentric network data. *BMC Public Health*, vol 13, p.784; accessed on 12 August 2-17 at: https://doi.org/10.1186/1471-2458-13-784

ABOUT THE AUTHOR

Joanna Jast is a Wall Street Journal Bestselling author, blogger, entrepreneur and self-appointed expert on human nature. She dreams of inventing a direct brain-computer interface so she can just upload/download knowledge and update her behaviour software in seconds. While awaiting the development of the appropriate technology, she works on improving the existing ways of absorbing knowledge and adapting to change.

Originally a medical doctor, Joanna is a mid-life career shifter with nearly 20 years' experience in psychiatry, psychotherapy and adult education. She puts her knowledge of neuroscience, cognitive psychology, and human nature into practice to help others accelerate their learning and personal change.

Her love for productivity, effectiveness and top-notch mental powers combined with her weak willpower and low threshold for boredom has resulted in a passion for finding effective shortcuts and well-proven strategies that really work.

Not Another F-ing Motivation Book is a result of Joanna's frustration with ineffective motivational strategies in the course of life-long experience in overcoming her natural laziness, bad habits and poor willpower to succeed in life.

Joanna is currently living in France juggling her business, writing, family commitments and continuous learning. In her spare time, she enjoys reading science-fiction and mystery novels, and indulging in her love of landscape photography.

If you want access to no-nonsense, realistic and practical advice on speeding up your success in professional and personal life visit www.theshapeshiftersclub.com.

Joanna is the author of *Laser-Sharp Focus* and *Hack Your Habits*.

ALSO BY JOANNA JAST

Laser-Sharp Focus. A No-Fluff Guide to Improved Concentration, Maximised Productivity and Fast-Track to Success.

(Buy the book on Amazon)

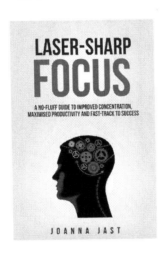

Unhappy with your productivity? Consumed by distractions, interruptions and wandering mind syndrome? Can't focus and concentrate? Tired of ineffective advice on how to improve your focus?

Whether you're a student, freelancer, entrepreneur (or wanna-be preneur), employee or anyone else dreaming of being able to snap into focus and stayed focused for however long you want, or wondering how to improve your productivity - this book is for you.

Discover how to focus, improve your concentration and memory, maximise your productivity and speed up your success with evidence-based strategies and proven tricks

This book is a practical, step-by-step guide on how to improve your focus and boost your productivity with a twist - it helps you identify what's not working first, so you can target your specific problems head-on, without wasting time and energy on stuff that's unlikely to work for you. And once your mental focus is laser-sharp your memory will improve and your productivity will soar, too.

The approach presented in this book unlike many other books on productivity, memory improvement or '100% focus', recognises and takes into consideration your individual situation, providing you with a roadmap so that you can check where you are and what you need to do to get where you want to be. This system will not only help you focus and concentrate, but as a result - will help you improve your memory, boost your productivity and - you will be able to adapt it to your life.

You will learn:

- How to identify what specifically is not working within your current 'focus system'
- What you can do to eliminate procrastination, minimise distractions, avoid interruptions, keep your mind on track, your emotions under control, and your body at top-level performance
- How to create a system that can adapt to your changing needs so that you focus on your job, whatever it is, whenever you need to and wherever you are.

To improve your focus, boost your concentration, and maximise your productivity grab a copy of *Laser-Sharp Focus* book now.

ALSO BY JOANNA JAST

Hack Your Habits. An Unusual Guide to Escape Motivational Traps, Bypass Willpower Problems and Accelerate Your Success.

(Buy the book on Amazon)

Tired of fluffy books on improving your habits? Sick of 'motivate yourself' advice? Short on self-control & willpower?

This book is for you - jam-packed with practical steps, tricks and strategies that will fit with your personality and your life, get you through motivational ups&downs, willpower outages, and 'life-got-in-the-way' obstacles, day-in, day-out taking you closer to your goal: a happier, wealthier, healthier you.

Until now, most strategies for habit formation relied on motivation and willpower. But in today's world full of temptations, self-restraint and self-discipline have become even harder. In order to build better habits, break old ones and transform your life you need a system not motivational fluff.

This book is for you if you:

- Have struggled with creating healthy or positive habits

- Experience a lack of self-control and battle every day to maintain your willpower
- Constantly try (but ultimately fail) to motivate yourself to change unhealthy habits

Learn how to:

- Design your positive habits the right way, so you start reaping the rewards from day one.
- Keep going even if your motivation and energy fails so you don't lose any forward progress.
- Minimise the impact of temptations so you never fail again.
- Implement small changes in your environment to make your new behaviours automatic much faster.
- Build a system that will help you effortlessly and quickly get to your habit goals so you can transform your life and achieve success faster.
- Create a powerful, lasting habit change that fits in with your personality and lifestyle and can adapt as you progress through life.

Dump ineffective strategies, embrace the power of *Hack Your Habits* framework and start building better habits today.

Grab a copy now.

83456623R00106

Made in the USA
San Bernardino, CA
25 July 2018